SPIRITUALLY WIDOWED WIVES

For Christian Women Married to Non-Christians or Men Who Neglect Spiritual Matters

By

Rosemarie D. Malroy

ISBN: 1-4033-2231-7 (e-book)
ISBN: 1-4033-2232-5 (Paperback)

Library of Congress Number 2002092069

This book is printed on acid free paper.

Printed in the United States of America
Bloomington, IN

Scripture taken from the HOLY BIBLE, NEW INTERNATIONAL VERSION® NIV®. Copyright © 1973, 1978, 1984 by International Bible Society. Used by Permission of Zondervan. All rights reserved

Cover painted by Rosemarie D. Malroy

1st Books - rev. 08/28/02

FOREWARD

This book is written for a special woman. God has given her a challenging ministry. He has called her to be a witness to her husband. It is a wordless witness that reflects God in her, hour-by-hour, day by day. It is one of the most difficult callings in the world for she is on the witness stand at all times.

The Sovereign Father, the gentle Jesus and the helper Holy Spirit are waiting in love to assist her. May they use this book.

Rosemarie D. Malroy.

Wives, in the same way be submissive to your husbands so that, if any of them do not believe the word, they may be won over without talk by the behavior of their wives, when they see the purity and reverence of your lives. (1 Peter 3:1 1 & 2)

HOW TO HAVE A BIBLE STUDY USING THIS BOOK

Either a small or large group of women can use this book as a Bible study

1. Set a designated time to meet.

2. Before the study assign the chapter in the book to be read.

3. When the group meets, read the designated Scripture. It will be helpful if one person has read some commentaries.

4. Discuss the Scripture verse by verse.

5. Answer the chapter questions together.

6. If members feel comfortable to do so, confess sins, and hold each other accountable.

7. Encourage each woman to ask forgiveness from her husband when she does something wrong.

8. End in prayer. Allow each woman to have the opportunity to pray.

ACKNOWLEDGMENTS

This book has taken over ten years to write. I wish to thank each one who helped—each in his unique way. Donna Goodrich helped edit, Jean Baxter did the graphics, Juanita Rolph wrote a chapter and encouraged me to write the book in the first place. Jewel Johnson gave suggestions; Betty Biesterveld and Sylvia Burke encouraged and the Fountain Hills Christian Writers Group has helped over the years.

I owe a great debt to Pastor Gerrit De Young who took time from his busy schedule to read my book and encourage me to continue my efforts. Shirley Miller lent me her poem. My niece and cousin helped, Dr. Dennis Hensley inspired me, Ingrid and Steve gave suggestions, and Sheri typed. And thank you Dr. Jay E. Adams for your helpful comments.

My husband, Fred, has been a great support as well as my children. Jason helped with his computer expertise and Eric and Sean encouraged and gave insightful comments. I thank my sisters, Sharon and Shirley, and my Mom for their love and for being there for me.

I thank also the women who have been an inspiration and example as they persevered. Some of them have had great difficulties being married to unbelieving men, yet they have trusted God.

The names of many helpers are not mentioned here. I am thankful for all the loving acts this book has brought about and may each contributor be blessed. Thank you dear God for your Word; may my readers be sanctified by it.

Rosemarie D. Malroy

CONTENTS

BALANCED BY A SYSTEMATIC STUDY OF THE BIBLE AND
BEING SENSITIVE TO THE HOLY SPIRIT

CHAPTER FIVE

YOUR HUSBAND CONSIDERS GOD A THIRD PARTY IN HIS
MARRIAGE. YOU FEEL TORN BETWEEN THE TWO.

CHAPTER SIX

HOW TO SIDESTEP ADULTERY AND DIVORCE.

CHAPTER SEVEN

AVOIDING MANIPULATION. FIVE RULES FOR
COMMUNICATION.

CHAPTER EIGHT

HOW TO BALANCE JUSTICE AND SUBMISSION.

CHAPTER NINE

VERBAL ABUSE AND HOW TO REACT. SIX RULES TO GUIDE
YOU. TEN SUGGESTIONS FOR
DEALING WITH A DIFFICULT MATE

CHAPTER SIXTEEN

HOW TO WITNESS TO YOUR HUSBAND WITHOUT PREACHING.

CHAPTER SEVENTEEN

A PARENT WHO FAILED. THE BASICS OF TRAINING.

CHAPTER EIGHTEEN

YOUR HUSBAND AND CHILDREN ARE UNDER THE COVENANT OF GOD.

CHAPTER NINETEEN

HAPPINESS IS BASED ON GOD.

Chapter One
FACING UP TO A BAD SITUATION

"I don't want to read the Bible, I can't stand to pray, and I'm not going to church anymore. I've decided I don't need religion. I have a right to choose what I want. I'm the one who takes care of myself, not God!"

Anger, hurt and fear gripped Lisa's soul. "Your timing is great." The bride broke into tears as she ran into the other room.

What am I going to do? she thought. *I believed Craig was a Christian when I married him. We went to church together and he told my pastor he was a Christian. How can he do this to me? Where did I go wrong?'*

Lisa trembled when she remembered the Scriptures that warned,

> Do not be yoked together with unbelievers. For what do righteousness and wickedness have in common? … What does a believer have in common with an unbeliever? (2 Corinthians 6:14a&15b)

She grieved over the thought that Craig would be judged for his unbelief. The Scripture said,

> Whoever believes in the Son has eternal life, but whoever rejects the Son will not see life, for God's wrath remains on him. (John 3:36)

The holy God's judgment was a fearful thing to Lisa.

As a new wife, Lisa suddenly found herself in a love-hate relationship with Craig. She loved him because he was her husband and she was emotionally bonded to him, but she hated him for deceiving her even though he might not have meant to do so. To her it didn't matter because the results were the same. She was crushed. Her dreams and hopes were shattered because she loved the Lord and wanted a solid Christian family.

The next day Lisa searched her heart more than she ever had before. "I tried to do everything right," she prayed. "God, why did you let him do this to me? Oh, Lord, help me. Why won't he believe?"

Dana was another woman in Lisa's church who was married to a man who rejected God and the Bible. There are different ways Christian women can become yoked to non-Christian husbands or men who neglect their spiritual relationship with God. Dana broke her mother's heart when she said, "Christian men are boring; I like men with action and excitement. I love Leon and I'm going to marry him."

Dana was like Samson who defied God by marrying an unbeliever. Samson came from a godly family and God called him to be a Nazarite, yet he fell in love with an exciting, sexy Philistine woman. When Samson's parents objected by asking why he didn't marry a godly girl, he ignored them and said, "Get her for me. She's the right one for me." (Judges 14:3b)

God let him go his sinful way, which ended in tragedy. Then Delilah, another Philistine woman, enchanted him. When Samson told Delilah the secret of his strength was his long hair, she betrayed him for silver and cut it off when he was asleep. It left him helpless in front of the Philistines and he was imprisoned and tormented.

Samson got into serious trouble by aligning himself with unbelievers. One sin led to another. But God used these events so Samson could destroy the cruel conquerors of the Israelites. When the Philistines brought him to the temple of their god Dagon to ridicule him and his God, the Lord gave him strength to pull down the pillars of their temple and he and 3,000 people died. In spite of the fact that Samson sinned in his love life, God used Samson for his own glory.

Like Samson, God was now using Dana to accomplish His purpose for her life. Wanting to serve God, she invited her cousin, Andrea, to church to hear the gospel.

"It was like a light going on," Andrea said. "When I heard Jesus died for my sins and that I could be sinless in God's sight, it was a great relief. When I went home to tell my husband, I thought he'd rejoice with me over the fact we can be forgiven and free. He said, 'Woman, what's the matter with you? Have you lost your senses?'"

"It's been very hard," she told Dana. "My husband is a wonderful man, but he doesn't have any desire to know God. I get lonely to talk to someone about spiritual matters. I have so many questions and sometimes it's hard knowing what is right to do."

"I know," said Dana. "Let's pray together. We can ask Lisa to come. I hear she is having a hard time too."

"How about me?" asked Jan.

"You're welcome to come but isn't your husband a Christian?" asked Dana.

"He claims to be," said Jan, "but he certainly doesn't act like one. He hasn't been to church for two months. He thinks only of business. I'm a spiritually widowed wife," she said bitterly.

Then correcting herself, she said, "I know I shouldn't be bitter, but when a man pretends to be a godly man and in his life he isn't, it is humiliating and I get very angry. I shouldn't say anything but sometimes I think I'll burst if I don't. It's as if I'm being a hypocrite."

"I think I understand," said Dana. "Come to our little prayer group, Jan. We can pray and learn together. God will help us grow as Christians so we can better cope."

> A woman married to a nominal Christian (a Christian in name only) or a questionable one—a backslider or one who is not actively a disciple of Christ—is a spiritually widowed wife also. Her husband is not the spiritual head of the family.

These four women have very different husbands and different problems, but they all have one thing in common. Their husbands are not taking the spiritual leadership in the home. The wife loves God and seeks to obey Him, but the husband has other priorities. These priorities in themselves may be good, but the husband doesn't seek to put God first in his life. There is no balance in a marriage when one partner is spiritually dead and the other spiritually alive. Each one teeters his own way—the unbeliever not performing his spiritual responsibilities and the Christian partner overburdened and unstable.

GOOD NEWS

There is good news, however. You don't need to be discouraged because God has given wonderful promises. He promises to balance and fill in for the unbelieving mate. HE PROMISES TO BE YOUR SPIRITUAL HUSBAND.

"For your Maker is your husband—the Lord Almighty is his name." Isaiah 54:5a

This book shows you how God can fill in for the unbeliever enabling you to have a balanced home. A balance happens when the believer allows God to guide the home. You, as a Christian, do this by reading the Bible and asking the Holy Spirit to help you understand and apply it. As your spiritual husband, God guides and directs through the Scriptures. He gives wisdom and balance for everyday problems and helps you in the ways you need. He gives you hope and promises to claim for your husband, yourself and your family.

TAKE HOPE. THIS BOOK SHOWS HOW GOD CAN FILL IN FOR THE UNBELIEVER ENABLING THE BELIEVER TO HAVE A BALANCED HOME.

UNBALANCED

What harmony is there between Christ and Belial?" (2 Corinthians 6:15)

Let me down!

There is no balance in a marriage when one partner is spiritually dead. Each one teeters his own way—the unbeliever not performing his spiritual responsibilities and the Christian partner overburdened and unstable.

BALANCED

God filling in for
the unbeliever

A guided Christian

"For everything that was in the past was written to teach us, so that through endurance and the encouragement of the scriptures we might have hope." (Romans 15:4)

"For your Maker is your husband—the Lord Almighty in His name." (Isaiah 54:5)

So let's begin on this spiritual journey together.

CHAPTER ONE
BIBLE STUDY AND DISCUSSION

Read the Scripture below. How is God your husband? Reread the Scripture and discuss how it can help you to be balanced by God.

"Do not be afraid; you will not suffer shame.
Do not fear disgrace; you will not be humiliated.
You will forget the shame of your youth
and remember no more the reproach
of your widowhood.
5 For your Maker is your husband—
The Lord Almighty is his name—
The Holy One of Israel is your Redeemer;
He is called the God of all the earth.
6 The Lord will call you back
as if you were a wife deserted and distressed in spirit—
a wife who married young,
Only to be rejected," says your God.

7 "For a brief moment I abandoned you,
But with deep compassion I will bring you back.
8 In a surge of anger
I hid my face from you for a moment,
but with everlasting kindness
I will have compassion on you," says the Lord your
Redeemer. (Isaiah 54:4-8)

You will keep in perfect peace
him whose mind is steadfast,
because he trusts in you. (Isaiah 26:3)

In the same way, the Spirit helps us in our weakness. We do not know what we ought to pray, but he Spirit himself intercedes for us with groans that words cannot express. 27 And he who searches our hearts knows the mind of the Spirit, because the Spirit intercedes for the saints in accordance with God's will. (Romans 8:26&27)

If any of you lacks wisdom, he should ask God, who gives generously to all without finding fault, and it will be given to him. (James 1:5)

When your words came, I ate them; they were my joy and my heart's delight, for I bear your name, O Lord God Almighty. (Jeremiah 15:16)

CHAPTER ONE QUESTIONS

1. What is the spiritual definition of a Christian? (John 3:16, Ephesians 2:4-5)

_____

_____

_____

2. What happens in a home where one partner is a believer and one is not?

_____

_____

_____

3. Name other Bible characters besides Samson who got into trouble because they married unbelievers. (Genesis 26:34-35; 1 Kings 11:1-3)

_____

_____

_____

4. The Christian's lifestyle and value system are often different from a non-Christian's. What might be some of the conflicts?

_____

_____

_____

5. Do you think God considers a woman or man inferior because they are married to an unbeliever? Describe what forgiveness entails. (1 John 1:9)

_____

_____

_____

6. What is a good verse to claim when you want an answer from
    God? (James 1:5)

    _____

    _____

    _____

7. Describe one area in which you would like to improve. Can
    fellow Christians help you with prayer?

    _____

    _____

    _____

Rosemarie D. Malroy

Chapter Two
GUIDED BY THE WORD—FINDING FORGIVENESS AND SHARING IT

Lisa struggled with the fact that Craig wasn't a Christian. Every day revealed the impact it meant on their lives. Finally, one day she came to God and said, "Dear God, I want to know why my husband isn't a Christian. Did I do anything wrong?" Lisa knew God speaks to His children through Scripture, but she did not expect to find the answer that day in her devotions in Genesis 24. Abraham had sent his servant to find a wife for his son, Isaac, from among his own people so Isaac wouldn't marry a heathen. The servant, upon arriving at Nahor, Abraham's hometown, asked God to show him the right girl. The Bible says,

> [The servant said,] "May it be that when I say to a girl, 'Please let down your jar that I may have a drink,' and she says, 'Drink, and I'll water your camels too'—let her be the one you have chosen for your servant Isaac. By this I will know that you have shown kindness to my master." ... Without saying a word, the man watched her (Rebecca) closely to learn whether or not the Lord had made his journey successful. (Genesis 24:14&21)

Lisa pondered the Bible story wherein the servant had waited and watched Rebecca closely. During her own courtship, Lisa had not waited to see if Craig's confession was true. She remembered her pastor's concern and recommendation that they postpone the wedding, but she felt everything

13

would be okay. Craig professed faith in Christ under her prodding, and she felt he'd go to church and learn. Craig wanted to start his new career with a wife and they couldn't wait.

The sudden realization stunned her. She had been too infatuated with Craig to "<u>watch him closely</u>" to see if God approved. She hadn't checked his words with his actions. If she had observed closely, she would have detected his lack of spiritual interest.

"Forgive me, Lord," she said. "Forgive me for not waiting and confirming Craig's confession of faith. Forgive me, also, for following my own emotions instead of your Word."

Finding forgiveness is a wonderful thing. You may not need to find forgiveness from God for sinning in the way Lisa did. Yet often there is bitterness and anger in hearts—especially when your mate reacts negatively to your faith. So it is important that you present all to God and ask His forgiveness.

Asking your husband to forgive you is important too. A secretary to a Christian counselor said her experience was that when Christian women confessed their sins to unsaved husbands, the office regularly had calls from the men. They asked why their wives had changed and were often willing to come for counseling. She believed confession of sinful responses was necessary even to unbelieving, harsh or antagonistic husbands.

You must also be willing to forgive your husband. Ephesians 4:32 says, "Be kind and compassionate to one another, forgiving each other, just as in Christ God forgave you." Remember, *forgiveness is a promise not to remember the sins of another.* Ideally, the person will come to you and ask forgiveness. Often, however, you have to go to the person and explain how you believe you have been injured before he will ask forgiveness. Then when you forgive, you are promising him you won't hold his offenses against him. Even though your husband may not ask to be forgiven, you owe it to him to tell him why you are concerned. That gives him the opportunity to ask for forgiveness. Many times there is a misunderstanding that can be cleared up if you tell what is troubling you.

As Lisa and her friends gathered for prayer and support, different questions were asked about forgiveness. "How can I forgive my husband if he doesn't even think he's doing wrong?" asked Jan. "If he doesn't ask for forgiveness, I can't grant it to him."

"You can have a loving and forgiving spirit—not counting his sins—and not being resentful," said Dana.

"I know that's true," said Lisa. "You know what helped me?"

"No, what?" asked Jan.

"Telling God exactly how I feel and how I think I'm being mistreated. Then I ask God to help me release the bitterness. It really helps. That lesson

I learned in the story of Hannah in 1 Samuel 1:1-20. It was my Bible devotion right when I needed it."

"I can't remember the story of Hannah," said Jan.

"Well," said Lisa, "Hannah was torn by bitterness. Peninnah, her husband's other wife, was tormenting her because she was childless. I thought that Hannah had a right to be angry and bitter. How terrible that her husband married Peninnah just because Hannah couldn't have children. And then—to have Peninnah be so malicious. The Bible says,

> And because the Lord had closed her womb, her rival kept provoking her in order to irritate her. This went on year after year. Whenever Hannah went up to the house of the Lord, her rival provoked her until she wept and would not eat. (1 Samuel 1:6-7)

I wondered when Peninnah continued to be so nasty, why Hannah didn't tell her off. That's what I'd have done, but she didn't."

> In bitterness of soul Hannah wept much and prayed to the Lord. And she made a vow, saying, "O Lord Almighty, if you will only look upon your servant's misery and remember me, and not forget your servant but give her a son, then I will give him to the Lord for all the days of his life, and no razor will ever be used on his head."

> As she kept on praying to the Lord, Eli, the priest, observed her mouth. Hannah was praying in her heart and her lips were moving but her voice was not heard. Eli thought she was drunk and said to her, "How long will you keep on getting drunk? Get rid of your wine." "Not so, my lord," Hannah replied. "I am a woman who is deeply troubled. I have not been drinking wine or beer; I was pouring out my soul to the Lord. Do not take your servant

for a wicked woman; I have been praying here out of my great anguish and grief."

Eli answered, "Go in peace, and may the God of Israel grant you what you have asked of him."

She said, "May your servant find favor in your eyes." Then she went her way and ate something and her face was no longer downcast. (1 Samuel 1:10-18)

Lisa said, "I realized Hannah was a woman like me. She was angry and depressed and deeply hurt. She didn't want to face her problem. Then I asked myself, 'what did Hannah do to break the vicious circle of bitterness and inertia?' She didn't change Peninnah. I hadn't changed Craig either. The answer was,

Hannah poured out her soul to the Lord.

"The difference was Hannah changed her attitude. She told God everything in her anguish and grief, venting all her feelings to Him. She got so emotional Eli thought she was drunk.

In bitterness of soul Hannah wept much and prayed to the Lord.

"So I did the same. I said, 'God I feel bitter against my husband. I hate myself and him too. Take my bitterness away. Help me to have a forgiving spirit. Please save him. Give me the hope to believe you will do so in your own time.'

"I admit I cried like Hannah. And do you know the tears seemed to melt the hardness of my heart. It was as if a great burden was taken away. I felt free at last. Then, like Hannah, I could cheerfully take on the day. That night I asked Craig to forgive me for my bitterness."

"I'll have to read the story of Hannah," Jan said. "Forgiveness is hard for me. How can you forget when someone does something that hurts you deeply? I can't forget it."

"I can't forget how Craig changed his mind about being a Christian," said Lisa. "Some days it just pops up in my mind."

"The way our pastor explained it," said Dana, "is that we can't forget but we can 'remember no more' like God does for us. 'Their sins and lawless acts I will remember no more.' (Hebrews 10:17) That means we don't need to bring the offense up to ourselves or others. We don't need to dwell on or repeat it. That is something we can do."

"I feel dishonest to say I forgive when Jack is in the midst of doing the very thing I say I forgive. That's just excusing sin."

"You're right. When a person is granted forgiveness, his part is to change and refrain from repeating the offense. However, we need a forgiving spirit toward a person when he doesn't want our forgiveness," Dana explained.

Jay Adams in his book *From Forgiven to Forgiving* describes people with a forgiving spirit, as,

"Grateful people who do remember the pit from which they were rescued. (Isaiah 51:1) They act neither shocked by sin in others nor superior to those in whom sin is found." (p. 112)

"That helps me a lot," said Trish. "Now I know what I'm to do. I'm not to be surprised or superior. With God's help maybe I can do it."

* * * *

Being forgiven and forgiving is a great blessing. It is necessary to commune with God. The father of the prodigal son is our example. With a loving heart he waited for his son to come back to him to ask forgiveness. Every day he prayed and watched for him. When the son returned, the waiting father received him with open arms and forgave him. He also pursued his oldest son when he was angry and refused to join the party. The father went out of the house to find him and ask him the problem. This gave the son the opportunity to express his jealous feelings.

> "My son," the father said, "you are always with me, and
> everything I have is yours. But we had to celebrate and be
> glad, because this brother of yours was dead and is alive
> again; he was lost and is found." (Luke 15:31&32)

19

What a loving picture to keep in mind as you daily practice a forgiving spirit. May God help you and may you too be ready to receive the errant one and confront the offender in love.

SEVEN STEP PLAN FOR DEALING WITH INJUSTICE

Has your husband treated you unjustly? Do you feel bitter toward him? Have you asked his forgiveness? Do you know how to be forgiving? Perhaps the following seven steps will help.

Go to God like Hannah and tell Him your problems and express your feelings. Don't hold back.

Tell God your faults and bitter attitudes; then confess them.

Ask God for wisdom. Check the Bible for principles you can apply to your problem. Take proper action.

1. Try to make amends with your husband.

2. Confess your sins to him and ask forgiveness if needed. Confront him with his sin.

3. Tell him of your concern and why you are upset.

4. Listen to his point of view.

5. Tell him how you feel. Give him the chance to ask your forgiveness.

   If he refuses to change and ask your forgiveness and you can do nothing, let God correct the matter and wait. Claim a special promise or the promises in Psalm 9:9-12. "The Lord also will be a stronghold for the oppressed, a stronghold in times of trouble." (Psalm 9:9)

Then:

6. Remember the pit from which you were rescued.

7. Act neither shocked by his sin nor superior to him.

In faith pray for him and wait for his change of heart, being ready to receive him.

CHAPTER TWO

BIBLE STUDY AND DISCUSSION

Read through and discuss each verse concentrating on the father's attitudes and actions. Do you need to copy the father? How?

11 Jesus continued: "There was a man who had two sons. 12 The younger one said to his father, 'Father, give me my share of the estate.' So he divided his property between them.

13 Not long after that, the younger son got together all he had, set off for a distant country and there squandered his wealth in wild living. 14 After he had spent everything, there was a severe famine in that whole country, and he began to be in need. 15 So he went and hired himself out to a citizen of that country, who sent him to his fields to feed pigs. 16 He longed to fill his stomach with the pods that the pigs were eating, but no one gave him anything.

17 When he came to his senses, he said 'How many of my father's hired men have food to spare, and here I am starving to death! 18 I will set out and go back to my father and say to him: Father, I have sinned against heaven and against you. 19 I am no longer worthy to be called your son; make me like one of your hired men.' 20 So he got up and went to his father. But while he was still a long way off, his father saw him and was filled with compassion for him; he ran to his son, threw his arms around him and kissed him.

21 The son said to him, 'Father, I have sinned against heaven and against you. I am no longer worthy to be called your son.

22 But the father said to his servants, 'Quick! Bring the best robe and put it on him. Put a ring on his finger and sandals on his feet. 23 Bring the fattened calf and kill it. Let's have a feast and celebrate. 24 For this son of mine was dead and is alive again; he was lost and is found.' So they began to celebrate.

25 Meanwhile, the older son was in the field. When he came near the house, he heard music and dancing. 26 So he called one of the servants and asked him what was going on.

27 'Your brother has come,' he replied, 'and your father has killed the fattened calf because he has him back safe and sound.'

28 The older brother became angry and refused to go in. So his father went out and pleaded with him. 29 But he answered his father, 'Look! All these years I've been slaving for you and never disobeyed your orders. Yet you never gave me even a young goat so I could celebrate with my friends. 30 But when this son of yours who has squandered your property with prostitutes comes home, you kill the fattened calf for him!'

31 'My son,' the father said, 'you are always with me, and everything I have is yours. 32 But we had to celebrate and be glad, because this brother of yours was dead and is alive again; he was lost and is found.'" (Luke 15:11-32)

CHAPTER TWO QUESTIONS

1. Describe how guilt can render a person ineffective.

   _____

   _____

   _____

2. Tell why you think it is important for a "spiritually widowed" wife to know she is forgiven by God. If she thinks she is unforgiven, how can that affect her marriage?

   _____

   _____

   _____

3. Do you think Lisa was blind to her own sin?

_____

_____

_____

4. What means did God use to give Lisa the answer?

_____

_____

_____

5. How can you be guided by God's Word?

_____

_____

_____

6. What is a good verse to claim when you want an answer from God?

_____

_____

_____

7. What did Lisa do before she was forgiven?

_____

_____

_____

8. If God has guided you specifically in your quiet time as you read the Bible, tell about it.

_____

_____

_____

Rosemarie D. Malroy

Chapter Three
MEETING WITH YOUR SPIRITUAL HUSBAND

A spiritually widowed wife does not have a husband to lead in matters of faith. Her husband is "dead" to God's ways. She needs God to be her spiritual husband—the leader of her family and her balance and security. In Isaiah 54:5a it says, "For your Maker is your husband." Perhaps you would like to read the text of Isaiah 54:4-8. Here it explains that God's Church does not need to be afraid or suffer shame because God is our husband. With deep compassion, He forgives us and will deal with us with kindness.

How is this done? How can God be your husband? How can you know God in such an intimate way you can talk with Him about your problems and expect Him to answer?

Melissa, a new Christian, stomped into the house and slammed the door. *Bob is terrible*, she thought. *I don't care if I yelled and screamed at him. He completely ignores me and does exactly what he wants. He treats me as if I'm not even a person but a pebble he can kick aside.*

Tears welled in her eyes. *Why didn't God punish him? He deserved it. When I became a Christian, he rejected God. I've tried hard to show him the way by being a good Christian wife.*

She remembered the scene outside. *What if the neighbors heard her? At church they saw her as a fine example of a devoted new Christian. They'd asked her to lead the women's group this month. They didn't know what an awful husband she had. Neither did they know how awful she was. How could she serve God when she felt so hateful? She'd like to get even with Bob—make him pay for hurting and shaming her. She didn't deserve it. She'd like to leave. She wished she could die.*

Melissa sat down and picked up her Bible for her quiet time. She turned to Jonah 4:1-4 and read the Scriptures for the day.

> But Jonah was greatly displeased and became angry. He prayed to the Lord, "O Lord, is this not what I said when I was still at home? This is why I was so quick to flee to Tarshish. I knew that you are a gracious and compassionate God, slow to anger and abounding in love, a God who relents from sending calamity. Now, O Lord, take away my life, for it is better for me to die than to live."

In the quiet of the morning Melissa thought about the story of Jonah. Jonah hated the Ninevites, because the people of Nineveh had been so awful to the Israelites. When God insisted he preach to them, Jonah ran away to Tarshish instead of obeying Him. He wanted no part of those terrible people being reconciled to God. God judged him for running away. Now Jonah was angry because God hadn't punished them—yet He punished Jonah for running off. In fact, God showed mercy to the Ninevites.

Melissa heaved a sigh. As she read the Scripture again, the words "slow to anger and abounding in love" leaped out at her.

"Oh, God, I am not slow to anger and I don't feel like abounding in love," she confessed. She read the Scripture again, and then another thought occurred to her and she wrote in her notebook:

"Jonah was an imperfect man, yet God used him. He had a bad temper and was angry because God showed mercy to the Ninevites and didn't give them what they deserved." Melissa then turned to the commentary and read what it had to say on this portion of Scripture.

God speaks to this foolish man [Jonah] to teach us to restore those that have fallen with a spirit of meekness, and with soft answers to turn away wrath. (Matthew Henry, Volume IV, p. 1299)

She thought a moment. The management class she was taking didn't teach this. It taught that a person had to be aggressive.

Melissa waited before God in the stillness. Her bitter emotions drained away as she felt God's presence. Then she wrote in her notebook: "God, I thank you that this shows me there is hope you may use me in spite of the fact I exhibit many of the sins of Jonah. Forgive me for my anger. Sometimes I want justice instead of mercy for Bob. Help me ask his forgiveness."

God helped Melissa understand her mistakes. He also encouraged her to lead the women's group. God's love surrounded her and she knew He was there for her. He was her spiritual husband. Perhaps "Morning Watch" will help you as it has other Christians.

Certain students at Cambridge in 1882 made a commitment to meet God every day for at least seven minutes. They called it their morning watch. This is how they divided their time.

MORNING WATCH

MINI QUIET TIME—SEVEN MINUTES*

½ minute   <u>WAIT</u> before God; pray for guidance.

4 minutes   <u>READ THE BIBLE</u>. Read slowly, expecting God to meet your needs. Start with one chapter or subject and read consecutively verse by verse. Read to understand.

2 ½ minutes   <u>PRAY</u>:

A Adoration—Adore

C Confession—Confess

T Thanksgiving—Thank

S Supplication—Ask

*<u>Seven Minutes with God</u>, Robert D. Foster, NavPress, P.O. Box 20, Colorado Springs, CO 80901.

God greatly blessed the Cambridge students. God will bless you, too, if you meet daily with Him. As a spiritually widowed wife, it is necessary to spend as much time as possible learning the mind of God and seeking His guidance. Make it a top priority to spend time alone with God. Who knows what God plans if you do?

Sometimes we need more time to spend with God. This outline for a 30-minute quiet time may be helpful.

OUTLINE FOR QUIET TIMES—30 MINUTES

Wait to quiet yourself so you can acknowledge God's presence. Praise Him.

Read Scripture three times:

> For general thought.
>
> For specific teaching or doctrine.
>
> For what God is trying to teach you.
>
> Pray back Scripture.

Read commentary on that Scripture.

Write down what God is teaching you.

Write down personal requests and thanks.

Pray daily requests for others and plan your day.

HINTS FOR BIBLE STUDY

1. <u>Have a set place and time</u>. It helps to have a special place where one plans to meet with God. Come prepared with several Bible translations, a spiral notebook, and Bible commentaries. When

you make this a habit, it becomes easier to do. It takes approximately one month to make an action a habit.

2. <u>Prepare and praise</u>. First, blank out all the confusions of the day and wait on God. Prepare your mind and heart to receive Him. Think of all that He has done for you. Marvel at Christ, the Creator of galaxies, willing to leave the Father and come to this earth to die for you. Think how He lived a perfect life that He gave to you so you would be acceptable to God. Remember how you depend on Jesus completely for your righteousness before God. Then praise Him and thank Him for your salvation. Forget self and bask in God's love and greatness.

3. <u>Read the Bible</u>. The next step is to read the lesson for the day. It may be only a couple of verses or it may be a chapter. Read the text three times. Then pray back the Scripture. For an example of praying back the Scripture use Zechariah 4:6b KJV. This verse is a great promise to do God's work. "Not by might, nor by power, but by my Spirit, saith the Lord of hosts." You can pray this verse so that its promise gets you through your current problem or project. It is amazing how God uses obscure passages to bring out truths you need.

4. <u>Read a commentary</u>. Sometimes you don't understand certain passages. That's where a commentary or other Bible help is needed. And sometimes when one thinks the passage is perfectly clear, a commentary will shed further light. Some use Matthew Henry's Commentary. Ask your pastor for other study helps which will fit your need. A daily devotional book that includes Scripture and its discussion makes a good starting place too. Make sure you also read the Scripture.

5. <u>You can write down what God teaches</u>. After reading the commentary, write down any specific lesson you learned in your notebook. See how that Scripture applies to your daily life. If you read Zechariah 4:1-10, you might record, "I need God's Spirit to help me react well to others today." Sometimes you will write more than a page. Other times it may be just a key sentence. Whatever you write, write for yourself.

6. <u>You can write down personal requests and thanks</u>. Now it's time to bring your problems to the Lord and ask for wisdom and help. List those problems that are weighing on your mind at the moment. Also list those things for which you're thankful.

Your notebook becomes your record of intimate experiences with God as you share goals, claim promises, confess sins, and review your life to determine where you have sinned and where there are areas of spiritual growth.

7. <u>Prayers and plan for the day</u>. In the front of the notebook list specific people and things for which to pray each day of the week.

Monday	Family members
Tuesday	Friends, acquaintances, children's teachers, co-workers
Wednesday	Pastor and wife and members of your church
Thursday	Other churches and missionaries
Friday	Government and goals

Now plan your day.

A quiet time keeps you close to God. It keeps you balanced by reviewing what God has done. This gives you faith to claim help for now and the future. It releases you from fear because you have a record of how He has helped you in the past. No matter what men may say, God has helped, is helping, and will help in the future.

CHAPTER THREE
BIBLE STUDY AND DISCUSSION

1. Find the verses which teach us we can trust God's Word for guidance.

_____

2. Paul complimented the Berean Church for something the members did. What was it?

_____

3. The Thessalonica Church was also commended by Paul. For what did he praise them?

_____

1. "And we also thank God continually because, when you received the Word of God, which you heard from us, you accepted it not as the word of men, but as it actually is, the Word of God, which is at work in you who believe." (1 Thessalonians 2:13)

2. "Very early in the morning, while it was still dark, Jesus got up, left the house and went off to a solitary place, where he prayed." (Mark 1:35) "But Jesus often withdrew to lonely places and prayed." (Luke 5:16)

3. "Therefore I tell you, whatever you ask for in prayer, believe that you have received it, and it will be yours." (Mark 11:24) "Then you will call upon me and come and pray to me and I will listen to you. You will seek me and find me when you seek me with all your heart." (Jeremiah 29:12-13)

4. Jesus Christ made an extra effort to regularly be alone with God. How did He do it?

_____

4. "For everything that was written in the past was written to teach us, so that through endurance and the encouragement of the scriptures we might have hope." (Romans 15:4) "If any of you lacks wisdom, he should ask God, who gives generously to all without finding fault, and it will be given to him. But when he asks, he must believe and not doubt, because he who doubts is like a wave of the sea, blown and tossed by the wind." (James 1:5-7) "For this God is our God for ever and ever; he will be our guide even to the end." (Psalm 48:14) "You guide me with your counsel." (Psalm 73:24)

5.

What promises can we claim which will help us set aside time alone with God?

_____

5.

"Now the Bereans were of more noble character than the Thessalonians, for they received the message with great eagerness and examined the Scriptures every day to see if what Paul said was true." (Acts 17:11)

6.

There is a possibility we won't feel like meeting with God. What are some verses which may help us?

_____

_____

_____

6. "So then, just as you received Christ Jesus as Lord, continue to live in Him, rooted and built up in Him, strengthened in the faith as you were taught, and overflowing with thankfulness." (Colossians 2:6) "I call on the Lord in my distress, and He answers me." (Psalm 120:1) "The law of the Lord is perfect, reviving the soul." (Psalm 19:7)

M	T	W	T	F	S	S	
							Week 1
							Week 2
							Week 3
							Week 4

Now it is a habit!

Chapter Four
THE BALANCING ACT

Even though you may not have a Christian husband to balance your thinking, <u>God will be your balance</u>. He will take the place of a husband who leads you spiritually. How does He do this? He uses His Word. In the Bible, truth is balanced by truth. God helps you recall these truths, if you systematically study the Bible to obtain a base of knowledge. Then the Holy Spirit shows you how to apply these truths in life. That is the balance.

Holy Spirit Reveals

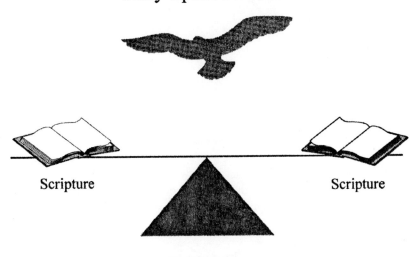

Scripture   Scripture

Balances

THE HOLY SPIRIT GIVES ANSWERS

BY HAVING US BALANCE ON TWO PRINCIPLES

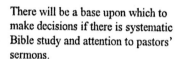

Bible Study	Daily Application

There will be a base upon which to make decisions if there is systematic Bible study and attention to pastors' sermons.

The Holy Spirit shows you how the scripture applies personally, often through daily devotions.

There are different ways to systematically study Scripture:

Genesis to Revelation (bird's-eye view)

By topic

By book

By chapter

> Jesus replied, "You are in error because you do not know the Scriptures or the power of God." (Matthew 22:29)

> But the man who looks intently into the perfect law that gives freedom, and continues to do this, not forgetting what he has heard, but doing it—he will be blessed in what he does. (James 1:25)

> And I will put my Spirit in you and move you to follow my decrees and be careful to keep my laws. (Ezekiel 36:27)

The <u>Thompson Chain Reference Bible</u> helps you to study a topic from Genesis through Revelation. It also outlines books and has many other helps. For an in-depth study Bible try the New Geneva Study Bible by Thomas Nelson Publishers.

Lisa's friend, Ruth, experienced an example of God's balance. Her husband's swearing had grown unusually bad. A loud volley of blasphemous words spewed from his mouth that early morning.

"Stop it! I can't stand your cursing," she scolded.

"Yeah," Donnie, their teenage son said under his breath to his mom. "Dad's mouth is like a curse on our home."

Donnie's words lay like a heavy weight on Ruth's heart. When she turned to her Scripture reading for the day, her eyes filled with tears. It was right there like Donnie said. Zechariah's vision of the flying scroll tells of God's wrath against all ungodliness, especially those who are wicked and profane. In Zechariah 5:1-4 the angel declares God hates men who swear.

> It [the curse] will remain in [the swearer's] house and
> destroy it, both its timbers and its stones. (Zechariah 5:4b)

Her commentary explained that the curse of the Lord is the judgment of God's Word. Scripture teaches that in the house of the wicked and profane sin rules. Therefore the curse is sin, which ruins houses and families.

Ruth shuddered. Was a curse upon her home? Were all her efforts to provide a Christian home in vain?

A heavy depression and foreboding filled her. She felt afraid. She also grieved for her husband's sin. But as she poured out her heart to God, the Holy Spirit brought to mind another verse from a recent sermon.

> For the unbelieving husband has been sanctified through his wife, and the unbelieving wife has been sanctified through her believing husband. Otherwise your children would be unclean, but as it is, they are holy. (1 Corinthians 7:14)

God highlighted His mercy to Ruth by the balance. His justice and hatred of sin were there, but His mercy covered all. That night she told her husband about the Scripture in Zechariah.

"Don, forgive me for being angry this morning. It really upsets me when you curse."

He was quiet for a moment.

"I'll try not to curse so much," he said. Even if Don reverted to his old way, Ruth knew she could cling to God's mercy for her home.

Not all non-Christian men have the same problem as Ruth's husband. But whenever one partner leaves God out of his life, the other needs special encouragement unique for that couple. The Holy Spirit encourages and gives the believer wisdom to find the balance for his life.

Remember, you are balanced by systematic study of the Bible and being sensitive to the Holy Spirit. Then the Holy Spirit can instruct you on specific problems through the application of God's Word.

WARY OF OUR DECEITFUL HEARTS

The balance can be broken. Debbie, who attends Lisa and Andrea's church, inadvertently uses Scripture for her own ends. She has two small children and the housework piles up until it seems impossible to control. She'll do anything to get out of the house. If her devotions include "<u>to look after orphans and widows in their distress</u>" (James 1:27b), she grabs the children and goes across town to visit a widow. Then she shops. She doesn't consider that her baby has a cold, there are no clean clothes in the drawers, and her husband will come home to a dirty house and no dinner. As far as she's concerned, she has done God's will and she tells her husband so.

Two of her friends spoke to her on the matter. They explained that she needs to learn she can't manipulate Scripture to meet her own moods. They lovingly showed her how she needs to be a woman who "<u>watches over the affairs of her household</u>." (Proverbs 31:27a) Otherwise she invalidates her own witness to her unsaved husband. One of the friends then offered to help her clean house as an encouragement to her.

God warns us of our deceitful hearts in His Word. He says that sometimes we may misuse Scripture. (Ezekiel 13:1-12)

He told Ezekiel, "Say to those who prophesy out of their own imagination: 'Hear the word of the Lord.'" (Ezekiel 13:2b) The false prophets practiced "positive thinking." They said there would be peace, and they didn't obey God and build a sturdy wall for battle like He told them to do. They built a flimsy wall and whitewashed it. Don't we do that too? Don't we whitewash our sins by not taking God's Word seriously so we can be guided aright?

Just like Debbie, we change the Scripture to mean what we want it to mean. Smiling and with a "positive attitude," we do what we want to do. We get out of doing the hard thing. We can't expect God's guidance when that is our attitude.

BALANCING ON GOD'S WORD

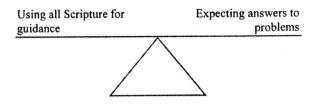

Using all Scripture for guidance

Expecting answers to problems

"The entrance of your words gives light; it gives understanding to the simple." (Psalm 119:130)

"For everything that was written in the past was written to teach us, so that through endurance and the encouragement of the scriptures we might have hope." (Romans 15:4)

UNBALANCED

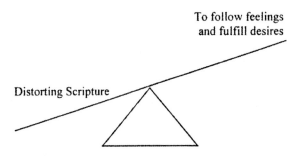

To follow feelings and fulfill desires

Distorting Scripture

"Woe to the foolish prophets who follow their own spirit and have seen nothing." (Ezekiel 13:3b)

"Have you not seen false visions and uttered lying divinations when you say, 'The Lord declares,' though I have not spoken?" (Ezekiel 13:7)

CHECKPOINTS FOR THE BALANCE

Because of man's deceitful heart, it is wise to have checkpoints. In major decisions you can ask your pastor for wisdom or ask friends for their counsel. God also uses husbands. You should ask your husband's opinion, even in spiritual matters. He has an eye to see the whole picture. You may get bogged down in details or are too close to the problem.

However, it isn't necessary to rush to others for every decision. In your quiet time God may let you know from Scripture when you need help from others. Sometimes He answers questions during daily devotions. The more you know His Word, the more the answers will flow, and you won't be fooled by a deceitful heart.

The importance of a daily quiet time cannot be over-emphasized. It makes usable Christians in Christ's church. Don't usurp your pastor's and friends' time. In fact the closer you walk with God, the more coping ability He gives you with the problems in marriage, and the more He will use you to help others.

A woman who has a particularly difficult marriage called a Christian friend. She was very upset.

"Do you remember Bill and Joanne, that attractive couple who lead in my church? They have a lovely home and well-mannered children. They seem to be the ideal couple."

"Yes," said her friend.

"Do you know what? They're getting a divorce. I always looked to them as a good example of a Christian marriage. Compared to theirs, my marriage is the pits; but they're the ones getting a divorce!"

"I can't believe it!"

"It's true. It makes me ask why I work to be a good wife when sometimes my husband doesn't even give me basic respect. Why keep my family together? If that couple can't make it, why should I try?"

"Wait a minute," said her friend. "What does the Bible say? What do you use to make your life's decisions—other people's actions or God's Word? And about this couple, what about their spiritual lives? Do either of them have a quiet time? Are they asking God to work in their lives to change them? Are they balancing on God's Word?"

CHAPTER FOUR
BIBLE STUDY AND DISCUSSION

Read the Scripture below. Discuss how God balances us. Who is speaking in the verses in John? In Ephesians how does Christ make the church holy?

Sanctify them by the truth; your word is truth. (John 17:17)

But when he, the Spirit of truth, comes, he will guide you into all truth. (John 16:13a)

15 If you love me, you will obey what I command. 16 And I will ask the Father, and he will give you another Counselor to be with you forever—17 the Spirit of truth. The world cannot accept him, because it neither sees him nor knows him. But you know him, for he lives with you and will be in you. (John 14:15-17)

Do your best to present yourself to God as one approved, a workman who does not need to be ashamed and who correctly handles the word of truth. (2 Timothy 2:15)

To make her holy, cleansing her by the washing with water through the word. (Ephesians 5:26)

CHAPTER FOUR QUESTIONS

1. What does it mean to systematically study the Bible?

   _____

   _____

   _____

2. What happens when we have great knowledge of the Bible but don't apply it?

   _____

   _____

   _____

3. What happens when we "wing it" and go by our emotions or "God's leading" and don't have knowledge of basic Bible truths? (Ezekiel 13:17)

   _____

   _____

   _____

4. What do you think it means to be part of the church of God?

   _____

   _____

   _____

5. What is basically wrong with usurping a pastor's and friend's time with too much talk? Proverbs 10:19

    _____

    _____

    _____

6. Where are reliable answers to life's problems obtained? (Romans 15:4)

    _____

    _____

    _____

7. How does God balance His hatred of sin with mercy?

    _____

    _____

    _____

8. How does Debbie's attitude toward her home and children discourage her husband from wanting a Christian walk?

    _____

    _____

    _____

Chapter Five
THE TRIANGLE

Now that you have your daily devotions and go to God for help and answers, one would think your husband would be grateful. After all, aren't you a sweeter and better wife? But often another problem rears its ugly head. It is the issue of the triangle.

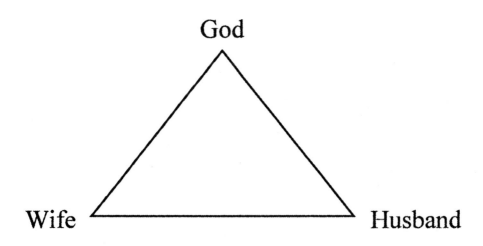

The triangle means the husband considers God a third party. As far as he's concerned, God has intruded into his life and is taking his wife's love and time. Even though he may consider himself an atheist, the fact remains his wife loves another whom she perceives to be God. The triangle produces conflicts which arise between a woman and her husband because of the woman's relationship and commitment to God. Subconsciously the man realizes he is competing with God for the attention of his wife. The more controlling a man is, the more conflict will arise.

However there is another, more subtle conflict when a couple is very loving and close. Sometimes the wife gives up trying to perform her Christian duties. She puts God on hold.

Ann sat at the back of the church so she could take out three-year-old Brad, if necessary, or go to her baby in the nursery. She watched the other couples with their children—fathers helping mothers with the needs of their families. She saw one father give his son a kiss and set him on his knee. How Ann wished her husband sat next to her. She missed him.

An elderly visitor seeing her alone, slipped in beside Ann. After the service they pleasantly spoke to one another.

"I'm glad to see you in church with your little ones," the stranger said. "It's so important to teach them the Bible when they are young."

Ann responded enthusiastically. "Brad and I read his Bible stories every night," she said. "He loves them."

"I'm so glad you do!" the woman replied. She paused and then said sadly, "I wish I had. Don't ever give up going to church or teaching your children God's ways."

"Weren't you a Christian?" asked Ann.

"Yes," said the old lady. "But I loved my husband very much and he didn't want to go to church. He wasn't interested in spiritual things."

"I understand," Ann said sympathetically.

"Don't make the mistake I did," said the woman. "We had a lovely life—no conflicts, and we did all kinds of fun things with the children. But John died and then I realized he didn't know God. I hadn't helped him at all. We had insulated our lives from the Lord. And my children—they don't know God either. I'm visiting one now. His son is on drugs."

Ann hasn't forgotten the grief in the old woman's eyes as she told her story. It helped her see that what is convenient, happy and easy isn't always the best. She learned a good Christian thinks of her children and what they will believe. She wants them to establish Christian homes so her grandchildren will know God. She looks ahead and realizes that the future of our churches and even our nation depends on godly homes.

When a Christian woman sees the great importance of being faithful to God and His church, it is difficult watching her husband sit home unseeing and uncaring, reading his paper or enjoying some entertainment. Instead of being bitter, a widowed wife has to be very careful she meets her husband's needs as well as serving God. Indeed that is one way to serve Him!

Early in Lisa's marriage she experienced trouble with this balance. Exciting things were happening at her church and she wanted to be a part of it. Her husband was dull in comparison to the Lord and His work. Craig felt the triangle.

"I don't know why you insisted we start this trip Sunday morning," Lisa said. She felt angry at him. He knew she taught Sunday school and Sunday morning was important to her.

"You aren't fun any more," he said. "Church, church, church, that's all you think about. It's about time we do something fun together."

She fumed. Why hadn't they done something together Friday or Saturday? Work, work, work, that's all he thought about. How come the big push for Sunday morning?

Their trip found them traveling in a forest. It was gorgeous country. A beautiful snow-covered mountain played peek-a-boo through the trees. Finally it disappeared and they lost themselves in the pines with only patches of blue above. These were stately pines—hundreds of years old. On a side road Craig stopped the truck. He took her hand and led her in the silent woods.

"Not many people have viewed such a sight," he said.

"Oh ..." The scene took Lisa's breath away. Huge pines towered above them. The floor of the forest was carpeted with grasses and wild flowers. Rays of sunlight sifted through the pine branches causing a shimmering light. A rustling in the stillness startled them. A mother deer and her fawn moved through the trees.

Craig looked at her. "I thought you would be a beautiful wood nymph," he said softly. "This is virgin timber—a virgin forest. Not like you," he said laughing. He kissed her and drew her down to the grass and flowers. Such a lovely bed. They were alone in this beautiful place. But why did she have this strange feeling in her heart?

Why did she feel like an adulteress?

In the triangle the man is not the only one who has problems. The woman also feels torn. She is torn between God and her husband. When her husband leads her away from doing what she believes right, she feels she has betrayed God. When she serves God, she feels guilty for leaving her husband. Such guilt can make her unable to enjoy life, her husband or the many blessings God has given her. She has to come to grips with her problem and find a balance. She has to trust God and make decisions.

Lisa learned she was doing too much in the church. She spent all day Sunday at different church functions, plus numerous activities during the week. Craig needed more attention. Her pastor showed her there were required Christian duties and optional ones. The one requirement, according to God's Word, was that she attend one worship service on Sunday, either morning or evening. "Let us not give up meeting together, as some are in the habit of doing, but let us encourage one another." (Hebrews 10:25a) Since her husband expressed resentment toward her church activities, she should spend as much time as she could with him.

Lisa talked things over with Craig. She told him she would cut some of her activities. She would make herself available to him when he wasn't working, except for Sunday mornings. That was the time she wanted to teach Sunday school and go to church.

When Lisa showed her earnestness in her request by cutting out most evening meetings and going with Craig after church, he respected her wishes. Over the years Saturday became the family day for outings and activities, and Craig didn't mind her bringing guests home for dinner after church.

BALANCING THE TRIANGLE

BALANCED

| Being a friend and com-
panion to spouse—meeting
his needs | Keeping up a relationship
with God and performing
Christian responsibilities |

"Her children rise up and bless her;
her husband also, and he praises
her..." Proverbs 31:28

"As each one has received a special gift,
employ it in serving one another, as good
stewards of the manifold grace of God."
(1 Peter 4:10)

"Not forsaking our own assembling
together, as is the habit of some, but
encouraging one another; and all the
more, as you see the day drawing near."
(Hebrews 10:25)

UNBALANCED

So immersing yourself in
the church and faith that
spouse's needs are not met

Forgetting Christian
responsibilities and with-
drawing from Christians

CHAPTER FIVE
BIBLE STUDY AND DISCUSSION

Read the Scriptures below. Make a list and discuss what God considers important to be a good wife.

> The Lord God said, "It is not good for the man to be alone. I will make a helper suitable for him." (Genesis 2:18)

> Your wife will be like a fruitful vine within your house; your sons will be like olive shoots around your table. (Psalm 128:3)

> May your fountain be blessed, and may you rejoice in the wife of your youth. 19 A loving doe, a graceful deer— may her breasts satisfy you always, may you ever be captivated by her love. (Proverbs 5:18-19)

> A wife of noble character is her husband's crown, but a disgraceful wife is like decay in his bones. (Proverbs 12:4)

> Houses and wealth are inherited from parents, but a prudent wife is from the Lord. (Proverbs 19:14)

> In the same way, their wives are to be women worthy of respect, not malicious talkers but temperate and trustworthy in everything. (1 Timothy 3:11)

> Wives, in the same way be submissive to your husbands so that, if any of them do not believe the word, they may be won over without talk by the behavior of their wives, 2 when they see the purity and reverence of your lives. (1 Peter 3:1&2)

> 3 The husband should fulfill his marital duty to his wife, and likewise the wife to her husband. 4 The wife's body does not belong to her alone but also to her husband. In the same way the husband's body does not belong to him alone but also to his wife. 5 Do not deprive each other except by

mutual consent and for a time, so that you may devote yourselves to prayer. Then come together again so that Satan will not tempt you because of your lack of self-control. (1 Corinthians 7:3-5)

Qualities of a Godly Wife

_____

_____

_____

_____

_____

_____

_____

_____

_____

CHAPTER FIVE QUESTIONS

1. The Scripture says God is your husband. "For your Maker is your husband, the Lord Almighty is his name." (Isaiah 54:5) Get into your husband's mind. Explain why he might feel jealous._____

_____

_____

2. What imbalances do you tend to lean toward? Is it easiest to neglect God or your husband?

_____

_____

_____

3. Each husband is unique. Each one is different in what is important to him. List what is important to your husband.

Things Important to my Husband

_____

_____

_____

_____

_____

_____

_____

_____

4. What are some of the Christian responsibilities we shouldn't

    neglect?

    _____

    _____

    _____

    _____

    _____

    _____

    _____

ASSIGNMENT

Write a list of your Christian responsibilities. Write another list of how you meet your husband's needs. Do they balance? What can you do to make the list more even?

Christian Responsibilities	Meeting Husband's Needs
1. _____	1. _____
2. _____	2. _____
3. _____	3. _____
4. _____	4. _____
5. _____	5. _____
6. _____	6. _____

Chapter Six
AVOIDING OTHER ROMANTIC ATTACHMENTS

"Sex without love leaves us cold," said the headlines in a USA paper. When mates are not loving, their partners seek love and sex outside the relationship, the article explained.

If you as a widowed wife feel genuine love is missing in your marriage, you, too, can become a statistic like the third of the population who commit adultery or over half who divorce.

Jessica professed faith in Christ after she married a rowdy young man. Life was not easy. He liked to go on drinking bouts with his friends and he neglected her. She felt unloved and left him for Dean who promised attention and romance. However that marriage was short-lived also. As soon as problems surfaced, she moved to romantic dreams and then to candlelight dinners with another.

Each time she made a break, she'd come back to her friends at church claiming she wanted to do better. She wanted a good marriage and happiness. However when the excitement of a new romance came her way, she forgot what she learned at Bible class. She wanted some fun. Jessica did not have a correct view of marriage. She didn't see marriage as a commitment but as a convenience with lots of romance. She did not understand love and what it requires. As Christ proved, love gives. It doesn't always receive.

It is interesting to observe that sometimes Christian women (or men) who are persecuted for their faith by their mates are the most vibrant and beautiful Christians. They sometimes have a depth of Christian maturity that their sisters who are cherished and loved by their husbands do not possess. Such a woman was Trish.

Trish trembled as she folded the note and stuffed it into her pocket. She didn't know why that little piece of paper could give her heart a jumpstart. She had been depressed lately. Mark, her husband, discouraged her. She was tired of trying to be a good wife to a man who didn't seem to care. His lack of love for the Lord put them in two different worlds. Mark ridiculed her love for God. He was very antagonistic about anything Christian, but his recent business trips gave her freedom. She loved the Lord so much that she had to do something to show it.

At church they needed help with the youth group. She was good at entertaining and all the kids loved her. She also admired Paul. He was so lonely since his wife died, but instead of feeling sorry for himself he worked with the young people. And that note he sent her—it couldn't hurt to look over Saturday's meeting with him at the mall.

Trish struggled to find the balance between loving another Christian and being pure in mind and heart concerning that Christian. She lacked perception to recognize dangerous situations and allowed her emotions to guide her. This hurt her relationship with Christ and tipped her balance so she lost control.

CHRISTIAN LOVE FOR EACH OTHER

BALANCE

"Love one another deeply." 1 Peter 1:22	Purity in mind and heart. Exodus 20:14, 17 Titus 2:5a

"Now that you have purified your-selves by obeying the truth so that you have sincere love for your brothers, love one another deeply, from the heart." (1 Peter 1:22)	"You shall not covet." (Exodus 20:17a) "To be self-controlled and pure." (Titus 2:5a) "You shall not commit adultery." (Exodus 10:14) "But I tell you that anyone who looks at a woman lustfully has already committed adultery." (Matthew 5:28)

Many people today view marriage as something they can discard if they feel unloved or if it doesn't meet their needs. God does not view marriage that way. He compares the relationship between husband and wife to that of Christ and the Church. (Ephesians 5:22-28)

Picture the people in your church. Do you see them all as perfect and wonderful? Yet they are Christ's Bride. Once they truly confess their faith in Jesus, He keeps them with all their warts, bad tempers, and whatever unloveliness they possess. They are His. And do they reject Christ when times get hard? If they are Christians, they won't. They may complain and rebel, but they belong to Christ forever.

The denigration of marriage in our society weakens people's understanding of the union of God's people with Christ. God does not like His pictures broken.

Remember what happened to Moses when God told him to speak to the rock and in a rage Moses hit it two times. (Numbers 20:2-12)

MOSES, THE PICTURE BREAKER

Moses led God's people for 28 years in the wilderness. They had gone through some tough times together. But, again, the people were angry. They said, "Why did you bring us up out of Egypt to this terrible place? It has no grain or figs, grapevines or pomegranates. And there is no water to drink!"

Moses and Aaron left the assembly and fell face down before God. And God told them what to do. "Take the staff, and you and your brother Aaron gather the assembly together. Speak to that rock before their eyes and it will pour out its water." (Numbers 20:8a)

Moses gathered the people together, but he was angry. "Listen, you rebels, must we bring you water out of this rock?" (Numbers 20:10b) Then in rage he took his staff and struck the rock two times and water poured out for the people. But God was angry. Moses, through his actions, destroyed the picture of the glory of God. Moses was to be only the mouthpiece of

God. He had no power. God was the One who gave the water. Moses destroyed the illustration of God the Giver and Moses the spokesman, and God told him it was such a serious sin that he would punish him by not allowing him to enter the Promised Land. Poor Moses died just before they entered the land flowing with milk and honey.

Christians today must be careful not to break God's picture—His picture of marriage personified by Christ and the Church. Divorce in order to remarry destroys God's picture even though it could appear to us that it would bring greater happiness. <u>Marriage is sacred in God's sight</u>.

The next time you are unhappy with your husband for being unloving to you, picture yourself as a beautiful bride without wrinkle or blemish. You are Christ's Bride and, in due time, you will be honored by Him for keeping your personal and corporate purity. (Ephesians 5:22-28)

TRISH'S LESSON

Trish and Paul "fell in love." They had a very difficult time sorting out the puzzle of their emotions and applying God's Word to their lives. Their love seemed so perfect—so pure—and their love for God made their being one. It took Trish quite a while to realize that she was committing adultery in soul and not loving God. "If you love me, you will obey what I command." (John 14:15)

After her experience Trish made seven rules to keep herself pure.

**Trish's Seven Rules
for Purity**

1. I will not spend time alone with another man nor depend upon his friendship.

2. I will not spend my time regretting my error in marrying a non-Christian nor compare my husband to another Christian man.

3. I will try to see the positive side of my marriage.

4. I will try to be a good companion to my husband.

5. I will try to be a good sex partner.

6. I will claim God's promises and depend on His help.

7. I will dress modestly and in good taste.

Questions to Ask Myself

1. Do I often feel unloved by my husband?

2. When I feel unloved how do I react? What do I say?

3. Do I make threats or insinuations that another could love me better?

4. Do I fantasize over another man?

5. Do I think if I were married to a Christian man, it would solve all my problems?

6. Is my husband my friend? Have I tried to cultivate his friendship even if it must be on his terms?

7. If I don't consider my husband my friend, who is my friend?

8. If my husband doesn't meet my needs, what do I do to protect myself from falling in love with another man?

9. Do I know Jesus is my Friend and Bridegroom?

10. Am I cultivating supportive relationships with other Christian women?

11. Am I becoming bitter and negative toward my husband because he isn't a Christian?

12. Am I using the difficulties I am experiencing in my marriage to cause me to grow as a Christian?

CHAPTER SIX
BIBLE STUDY AND DISCUSSION

Read and discuss each verse. When we believe Christ is our spiritual groom, how does that help us to be pure?

> Since, then, you have been raised with Christ, set your hearts on things above, where Christ is seated at the right hand of God. 2 Set your minds on things above, not on earthly things. 3 For you died, and your life is now hidden with Christ in God. 4 When Christ, who is your life, appears, then you also will appear with him in glory.
>
> 5 Put to death therefore, whatever belongs to your earthly nature: sexual immorality, impurity, lust, evil desires and greed, which is idolatry. (Colossians 3:1-5)

CHAPTER SIX QUESTIONS

1. God means for a Christian marriage to reflect the relationship of Christ and the Church. Why is it wrong for a Christian woman, even though she is married to a non-Christian, to break that picture?

    _____

    _____

    _____

2. What happened to Moses when he broke the picture God wanted him to portray?

_____

_____

_____

3. It is certain that your husband doesn't love you like Christ loves the church. Even if he is a Christian, he doesn't have the capacity to love like Christ. What should be your response to your imperfect husband?

_____

_____

_____

4. How do you think fantasy could be used as an act of adultery? (Matthew 5:27, 28)

_____

_____

_____

5. How can persisting in fantasy lead a woman astray?

_____

_____

_____

6. Why should a Christian woman exercise discipline in the matter of fantasy?

_____

_____

_____

7. God's Word can be very difficult to follow. What is more important to you—God's Word or your emotions?

_____

_____

_____

8. How long does God's Word last? How long do your emotions last?

_____

_____

_____

We have discussed in earlier chapters that Christ promises to meet your spiritual needs when your husband fails you. When you feel unloved, have you experienced Christ's love to you through
His Word?

_____

A Christian friend?

_____

The church?

_____

Describe your experience.

_____

_____

_____

9. God forgives us of sin. Can you also trust Him to keep you from

    sin?

    _____

    How will He do that?

    Pray that He will keep you holy and blameless. (2 Peter 1:3, 4)

CLAIM THE PROMISES

His divine power has given us everything we need for life
and godliness through our knowledge of him who called us by
his own glory and goodness. Through these he has given us his
very great and precious promises, so that through them you may
participate in the divine nature and escape the corruption in the
world caused by evil desires (2 Peter 1:3,4).

Rosemarie D. Malroy

Chapter Seven
HUSBAND MANIPULATION

A Christian woman married to a spiritually rebellious man can become completely frustrated. She deals with spiritual matters that are intangible. Her spouse views her spirituality as something superfluous, inconvenient or downright "kooky." In her frustration a woman may resort to manipulation.

Lisa lay the worn pamphlet down. It was yellow with age, but maybe it would work. She was desperate. Why not try this approach to bring her husband to Christ. The pamphlet taught the nutcracker approach. Love motivates to submit. If she submits to her husband in <u>all</u> things, it says her submission would be like the vice of a nutcracker—cracking the shell of Craig's unbelief.

She felt steely. Any man who would not go to the Christmas program to see his four-year-old son participate needed to be cracked.

Craig breezed in late for dinner. "Sorry I'm late," he said. He looked a little surprised when Lisa didn't scold him.

"Saw Roger," he continued. "He's lonely. I invited him to dinner next week sometime."

Lisa started to protest. Next week was the week before Christmas. The baby was teething too. Besides Roger deserved to be lonely. He was the one who committed adultery and started the trouble.

Lisa pigeonholed her protests and answered sweetly, "Yes, dear." Over the week "yes, dears" vibrated throughout the household. Lisa tried her best to love through submission. But instead of Craig being grateful, he seemed irritated.

The night before the Christmas program, the climax came.

"Lisa, fix these pants right now," Craig commanded. It was an unreasonable request. Lisa sighed. She lay the baby down, letting her cry, and got up to fix Craig's pants. He looked at her. "I can't believe you," he said. He grabbed the nearby teddy bear and in a rage threw it on the floor.

"Pick it up," he yelled. "Pick it up and be the doormat you want to be. I can't stand women who are doormats."

"You're terrible," Lisa cried. "I've tried my best to be a good wife."

"A good wife?" Craig exploded. "You aren't a good wife. You're trying to manipulate me. Well, it won't work. I'm not going to the Christmas program."

Craig rightly interpreted Lisa's manipulation technique. He still, however, didn't understand her desire for support and the need for a spiritual man.

Perhaps you are more gifted at manipulating your husband than Lisa. Perhaps for you it works. But deep down a man knows when he is being manipulated and he resents it.

A woman who waits until God works in her husband's heart is the woman who will be blessed. But there are constructive things she can do while she waits.

One of the most important things to learn is to communicate well. To do that it is necessary to break down communication barriers. What is a communication barrier? A communication barrier waves a red flag that says ...

I am:

moralizing

preaching

giving a guilt trip

arguing

lecturing

The red flag says <u>I am going to convince you that my way is right and you are wrong</u>.

If you can be aware of these red flags and avoid them, you can better communicate as you work through a problem. At least you will be heard and have less conflict.

<u>In order to communicate, your job is not to convince but state the problem or your desire</u>.

As a woman, sometimes you take other alternatives that fit your personality. You may choose to:

1. Lash out in anger

2. Rage or tantrum

3. Pout

4. Hide the frustration and not let on that you are angry

Any one of these choices is easy to do, but each one hinders communication. "Diplomacy is the answer to communication."

How can a hurt, demoralized, frustrated woman use diplomacy? It can be done through practice, perseverance, and using the following five steps.

FIVE REASONABLE RULES FOR COMMUNICATION

1. <u>Set the Stage</u>

In order to resolve conflict, the stage needs to be set. A Christian wife sets the stage by making her home a lovely place to be. She reserves confrontation for important matters and does not try to preach. She is a loving mate who makes her husband feel she is on his side. First Peter 3:1-2 is God's description of setting the stage.

> Wives, in the same way be submissive to your husbands so that, if any of them do not believe the word, they may be won over without talk by the behavior of their wives, when they see the purity and reverence of your lives.

A woman's life can be pure and reverent when she learns to communicate properly even though she doesn't talk about spiritual matters.

2. <u>Introduce the Problem with Love</u>

The introduction is positive. It begins your conversation with saying something good about the other person or showing some understanding of that person's needs.

"Craig, I know you have been working hard at your job and like to relax Sunday nights, but I believe we need to support our son. You are an important person in his life."

The introduction is not:

    a.   Defensive. "I know I'm doing right by taking our son to Sunday school. Why don't you support us?"

    b.   Accusing. "Craig, you don't care about us."

    c.   Expressing hurt. "I feel terrible when you don't go with us."

    d.   Self-justifying. "I'm the only one who really cares about our son."

3. <u>State the Problem as You See It</u>

It is important to let the other person know you are stating your opinion. No matter how right you are, this helps to come across as respectful and not dictating or bossy. It leaves the possibility that you could be wrong so there is room for further discussion.

"Craig, I know you have been working hard on your job and like to relax Sunday nights, but <u>I believe we need to support our little son</u>. You are an important person in his life. Even if you don't think Sunday school is necessary, it means so much to him to have you attend the Christmas program. I feel discouraged and unloved when you don't support us. Please come with us."

4. <u>State How You Feel</u>

In the example Lisa said, "I feel discouraged and unloved when you don't support us." It is important for your mate to understand that the issue at hand is very important to you even though you are acting in an adult manner. However, don't put the blame for your feelings upon your spouse. Don't say, "You hurt me." Say, "I'm hurt." Be sure it is your feelings you are expressing and not a thought. "I feel you should go," is expressing a thought, not a feeling.

You are responsible for your own feelings. Even though another person elicits your feelings, your feelings are a reaction to him. You are responsible for your reactions as well as your actions. God will help you in this area. Talk to Him about it during your quiet time and prepare for communication.

When you express your feelings, you are honest with your mate and let him understand you better. But you are not shifting the blame for your feelings upon him, which destroys communication.

5. <u>State What You Want</u>

In the example Lisa stated it simply, "Please come with us." She didn't use any manipulation, and she approached her husband in a non-spiritual way, so he could understand the needs of the family.

Now comes the hard part. What if Craig still refuses to go? What if you use the Five Reasonable Rules to Communicate and you get rebuffed? Sometimes it isn't easy but if you keep your long-term goals in mind and continue one step at a time, you won't get so emotional and negative and will be able to forge onward. Here are five more suggestions to help you.

REACTIONS TO A NEGATIVE RESPONSE OR UNREASONABLE BEHAVIOR

1. Go to the Lord and tell Him all your troubles.

2. Realize your mate is responsible for his actions.

3. Realize you are not responsible to see that he does right.

4. Try to look at the whole picture.

5. Trust God for help and make the best of the matter.

If Craig refused to go and didn't object, Lisa could make arrangements to stop at her son's favorite restaurant for a soda with some friends and make it a happy time.

Sometimes if a spouse reacts negatively, it is necessary to state the consequences. Remember, a consequence is not a punishment, nor is it trying to get even or manipulate. <u>It is simply stating what you will have to do under the circumstances</u>.

"If you aren't home by 6:30 p.m., we will have to go on without you."

CHAPTER SEVEN
BIBLE STUDY AND DISCUSSION

If possible, read the book of Esther. Then read the following and discuss. Do you think Esther practiced the Five Reasonable Rules for Communicating? If she did, tell how. Review the steps.

> On the third day Esther put on her royal robes and stood in the inner court of the palace, in front of the king's hall. The king was sitting on his royal throne in the hall, facing the entrance. 2 When he saw Queen Esther standing in the court, he was pleased with her and held out to her the gold scepter that was in his hand. So Esther approached and touched the tip of the scepter.
>
> 3 Then the king asked, "what is it, Queen Ester? What is your request? Even up to half the kingdom, it will be given you."
>
> 4 "If it pleases the king," replied Esther, "let the king, together with Haman, come today to a banquet I have prepared for him."
>
> 5 Bring Haman at once," the king said, "so that we may do what Esther asks."
>
> So the king and Haman went to the banquet Esther had prepared. 6 As they were drinking wine, the king again asked Esther, "Now what is your petition? It will be given you. And what is your request? Even up to half the kingdom, it will be granted."
>
> 7 Esther replied, "My petition and my request is this. 8 If the king regards me with favor and if it pleases the king to grant my petition and fulfill my request, let the king and Haman come tomorrow to the banquet I will prepare for them. Then I will answer the king's question." (Esther 5 1-8)
>
> So the king and Haman went to dine with Queen Esther, 2 and as they were drinking wine on that second day, the king again asked, "Queen Esther, what is your petition? It

will be given you. What is your request? Even up to half the kingdom, it will be granted."

3 Then Queen Esther answered, "if I have found favor with you, O king, and if it pleases your majesty, grant me my life—this is my petition. And spare my people—this is my request.

4 For I and my people have been sold for destruction and slaughter and annihilation. If we had merely been sold as male and female slaves, I would have kept quiet, because no such distress would justify disturbing the king." (Esther 7:1-4)

Esther again pleaded with the king, falling at his feet and weeping. She begged him to put an end to the evil plan of Haman the Agagite, which he had devised against the Jews. 4 Then the king extended the gold scepter to Esther and she arose and stood before him.

5 If it pleases the king," she said, "and if he regards me with favor and thinks it the right thing to do, and if he is pleased with me, let an order be written overruling the dispatches that Haman son of Hammedatha, the Agagite, devised and wrote to destroy the Jews in all the king's provinces. 6 For how can I bear to see disaster fall on my people? How can I bear to see the destruction of my family?"(Esther 8: 3-6)

CHAPTER SEVEN QUESTIONS

1. List the Five Reasonable Rules for Communication.

   a. _____

   _____

   b. _____

   _____

   c. _____

   _____

   d. _____

   e. _____

2. In practicing these rules in your home:

   a. Does your husband feel you are on his side?

   _____

   b. Have you stated something positive about him or expressed understanding of his viewpoint?

   _____

   c. Have you stated the problem as clearly as possible?

   _____

   d. Did you let him know how you feel?

   _____

    e.   Did you let him know what you want?

_____

EXERCISE

Write out how you would approach your husband on a specific problem using the Five Rules for Communicating.

1. _____

   _____

   _____

2. _____

   _____

   _____

3. _____

   _____

   _____

4. _____

   _____

   _____

5. _____

   _____

   _____

Chapter Eight
WIFE MANIPULATION

While a woman avoids manipulating her husband, she also shouldn't let him manipulate her. Men control women through fear, guilt, bad behavior, and the woman's emotions.

Kirsten ran her fingers through her hair. The lecture from her husband in his cool, even voice continued. She felt like screaming, but she didn't have the energy. Yes, Harold was right. The house was a mess, but three-year-old Jessie had a cold and the baby needed nursing every four hours.

"If you'd only rinse off the knife after you use it, wipe it, and put it away, you wouldn't have such a mess," he said.

Kirsten edged toward the door. She heard the baby crying and knew it was time to feed her, but Harold still talked. He showed disgust for her inabilities. She didn't dare go to Bible study tonight even though Harold said he would watch the children. She hadn't gone anywhere for two weeks. He even did the grocery shopping. She felt like he surrounded her world, fencing her in to endless housework and babies. Yet he was right. Her house didn't measure up.

A man can control a woman through guilt. A woman needs to recognize when she is being manipulated in this way. Kirsten didn't.

Kirsten, a devout Christian, took 1 Peter 3:1 seriously:

> Wives, in the same way be submissive to your husbands so that, if any of them do not believe the word, they may be won over without talk by the behavior of their wives, when they see the purity and reverence of your lives.

But because Kirsten fell into the trap of her husband's control and manipulation, she lost sight of her purpose.

The purpose of submitting was to glorify God, honor her husband and gain his respect. Kirsten was not submitting herself to her husband; she was abasing herself. There is a difference. <u>Submission suggests yielding and abasing suggests a voluntary loss of dignity, which results in degrading oneself.</u> She was not taking responsibility for decisions but giving her mind and will to him. Because she allowed her husband to dominate and manipulate her, she was losing his respect. She became a nonperson in his eyes and she was paying a heavy price. She was getting so depressed, she didn't cope.

Finally in desperation, Kirsten ran off to a friend's home, leaving her children and husband. She had lost all self-respect and neared a mental breakdown. But God is gracious. The friend got an elder to talk to them both and counsel them.

Amazingly, Harold listened and gave Kirsten help and some understanding. She learned not to allow him to manipulate her through guilt. She did her very best with her home. She also recognized her own needs and met them even though all her work was not finished. Her energy level increased, and Kirsten developed into a woman her husband respected.

Is your husband manipulating you? What red buttons does he push? Does he push the right ones so you react poorly, and then he can justify his bad behavior? If he does, you need to be "as shrewd as snakes and as innocent as doves." (Matthew 10:16b)

To be shrewd and innocent, we need to balance justice and submission. What does it mean to balance justice and submission? First determine what is just in order to combat the man who manipulates. Don't give way to fear but decide what is right in your circumstances. Include your husband's needs as well as your needs and your children's needs.

Cathy and Paul made an agreement that if Paul went fishing for one weekend, Cathy could attend a woman's retreat later in the month. Before she left for the retreat, Paul sprained his ankle. He tried to lay a guilt trip on Cathy for leaving him and the kids. He was trying to keep her home, using his ankle as the excuse.

Cathy realized what Paul was doing. She weighed the needs of each family member. She realized Paul physically could get along quite well without her, and it would be good for her teenagers to help Dad. However, she knew that it meant a lot to Paul to have her show she cared about him. She decided to take the opportunity to show him how important he was in her life. It would have been just or right for Cathy to go to the retreat, but she decided to show her husband love and meet his emotional needs. It was her way of letting God's love flow through her to her husband. It was a step of faith on her part.

If Cathy was having difficulty coping at home at that time, maybe then it would be wise for her to attend the retreat to get a fresh perspective. Each incident is different. An individual needs guidance from God.

Submission does not mean allowing your mate to manipulate you. A submissive spirit creates a setting for the Holy Spirit to work, for communication to take place, and for prayers to be answered. Manipulation eliminates justice and allows a woman to be used. It also can create fear, which keeps a woman from making wise decisions and from acting courageously or with dignity. Don't allow your husband to manipulate you. Rise above him. Balance justice and submission.

UNBALANCED

Causing Unnecessary Contention

Abasing yourself: fearing

NOT ALLOWING MANIPULATION

BALANCED

Being just to yourself,
your husband and children.   Being submissive

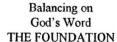

Balancing on
God's Word
THE FOUNDATION

"To do what is right and just is more acceptable to the Lord than sacrifice." (Proverbs 21:3).

To show inner strength, wisdom and the desire for justice.

"Wives in the same way be submissive to your husband." (1 Peter 3:1)

To show purity and reverence which helps your husband be drawn to Christ.

CHAPTER EIGHT
BIBLE STUDY AND DISCUSSION

Read the Scripture and then use the questions at the bottom for discussion.

> Wives, in the same way be submissive to your husbands so that, it any of them do not believe the word, they may be won over without talk by the behavior of their wives, 2 when they see the purity and reverence of your lives. 3 Your beauty should not come from outward adornment, such as braided hair and the wearing of gold jewelry and fine clothes. 4 Instead, it should be that of your inner self, the unfading beauty of a gentle and quiet spirit, which is of great worth in God's sight. 5 For this is the way the holy women of the past who put their hope in God used to make themselves beautiful. They were submissive to their own husbands, 6 like Sarah, who obeyed Abraham and called him her master. You are her daughters if you do what is right and do not give way to fear. (1 Peter 3:1-6)

1. In 1 Peter 3:1 what is the purpose for a woman to be submissive to her husband?

2. Sarah was given as an example of a woman who obeyed her husband and submitted to him. Yet in Genesis 21:10 it says, "And she said to Abraham, 'Get rid of that slave woman and her son, for that slave woman's son will never share in the inheritance with my son Isaac.'" Later in verse 11 God said, "Listen to whatever Sarah tells you, because it is through Isaac that your offspring will be reckoned." Why wasn't Sarah

condemned by God for ordering Abraham to get rid of Ishmael?

(Genesis 21:9-12)

3. Did Sarah consider the past, present, and future?

4. In your life is there a godly purpose in your submission? Are

    you doing it to show respect? Express love? Lead your husband

    to Christ?

5. What are your reasons for submitting?

CHAPTER EIGHT QUESTIONS

These questions need to be handled carefully. Be sure not to slander.

1. Have you thought through your actions to see if you are being manipulated through fear?

    _____

    _____

2. Are you eliminating justice by heeding unreasonable demands?

    _____

    _____

    Are you being manipulated by the use of guilt? _____

    Bad behavior? _____ Your emotions?

    _____

    _____

3. Do you have any "red buttons" that can be pushed regularly so that you will react negatively and he can get his way because of your guilt? What are some of your red buttons?

    _____

    _____

    _____

    _____

4. What examples do you know of men manipulating women? Describe.

_____

_____

_____

5. Can you see any parallels in your life?

_____

_____

6. Do you understand the difference between being abased and being submissive?

_____

_____

7. Do you respect yourself for your reactions? Explain.

_____

_____

Rosemarie D. Malroy

.

Chapter Nine
DEALING WITH ABUSE

Abuse in marriage is common. Where else can a spouse get even with the world and "get away with it?" Men and women in their sinful nature tend to take out their frustration and anger on the people closest to them. Mates are convenient and they often overlook bad behavior.

In this chapter we will be dealing with abuse other than physical abuse. Physical abuse will be dealt with more fully in Chapter Ten. Abuse can be defined as to mistreat, reproach with coarse and insulting language, or to harshly belittle or put down.

It is interesting to note that when God tells Christian women how to act when they are married to an unbeliever, he follows that advice with instructions on how to react to abuse. (1 Peter 3:8-17)

In dealing with abuse, God's way is very difficult. It goes against our grain and against everything we are taught in our society. The truth about abuse is that we can't control the one who is giving us the abuse. Neither can we change him. Only God can do that. However, we can change ourselves, and God is very pragmatic in telling us what to do. He promises us a blessing if we obey Him.

"But even if you should suffer for what is right, you are blessed." (1 Peter 3:14a)

The following six commands help you avoid abuse and gain God's blessing. It should be made clear that the suggested approaches following the commands have helped individual women. However, the personalities of you and your husband are unique. In your quiet time ask God to reveal to you your strengths and weaknesses. If you are a strong, verbal woman, maybe you should work harder to be gentle and quiet. If you are a gentle, quiet woman, maybe you should be stronger and more verbal. The commands are clear. How to implement them takes wisdom and dependence on God.

When we receive abuse, one of the first things God tells us to do in 1 Peter 3:9 is:

1. "Do not repay evil with evil or insult with insult, but with blessing."

Can you imagine a harder command? And yet it is a command from the dear Lord who has your best interest at heart. It is a command that requires the grace of God to obey. With a troubled man, it may be something you have to struggle with daily. So you wear down. But God knows. He will help you find a way to stand even though you probably will fall many times. He did so with Nora.

Nora dreaded her husband's return from work. Each night he stormed into the house finding something to yell about.

"Where's the mail? Give me my mail. I don't want you shuffling through it. How come it isn't all right here?!"

Nora usually responded by trying to reason with him or give him a lecture, which would make him angrier. Sometimes she'd yell back and put him in his place. Usually that started a round of insults, and by dinner they'd hardly be speaking.

Tonight she'd try something new. She read an article in one of the women's magazines that told how certain men could be quieted by a word of sympathy.

As usual Russ stormed in the door angry.

"Get that dog out of our yard. If your kids would keep the gate closed, we wouldn't have the neighbor's mutts in our yard. Can't you ever keep order?"

Nora swallowed her anger and said sympathetically, "It's a hot day. You must be really tired. Sit down and relax and I'll get you a glass of lemonade and tell the kids to take care of the dog." To her surprise the anger left his face and he gratefully accepted the cool drink. In the days that followed Nora could hardly believe that all her husband needed was a word of sympathy to calm him and make him agreeable.

When she studied 1 Peter 3:8 she realized such advice was not new. It read, "Finally, all of you, live in harmony with one another; <u>be sympathetic</u>, love as brothers, be compassionate and humble" (emphasis added).

Another pragmatic way to rebuff insults is to use nondefensive responses. With nondefensive responses you don't make excuses or apologize. You humbly agree with your spouse. In that way he has nothing to fight about.

"You're right, dinner isn't ready. I don't blame you for being upset when you're tired and hungry. Tomorrow night we'll probably do better. Let's eat out tonight."

Not to excuse or defend yourself is sometimes the best way to keep peace.

Forbearance is another way to overcome conflict. The word "forbear" means to control yourself when provoked. It doesn't mean to "stifle" yourself; it means to conquer emotions. "Let it all hang out" is the modern command, but when you forbear, no insult can do you harm because you don't allow it to irritate you. An insult can harm you only when you allow yourself to become angry or hurt. You can get the victory over it, utterly disarm it of power to do you injury by holding yourself superior to it. To keep silent when provoked is often the answer in avoiding abuse if you don't use it as a weapon or as a means to avoid communicating.

Some women make their husbands angry by their cold shoulder treatment or superior attitude. Forbearance doesn't do this. It does not harbor resentment, but rises above it. It is a loving way to cover up your partner's bad temper and protect yourself. Forbearance thus becomes a perfect shield, which protects you from all the cruelties and wrongs of life. To forbear requires humility, self-discipline and God's help, but it can make a happier life.

Jim, a man who was very controlling, resented his wife going out with her friends for lunch. When she asked him how she looked, he said, "You look like a fat pig."

Instead of reacting to the insult, Lin said, "That's too bad." She then put it out of her mind and had a good time with her friends. She had not let him control or hurt her and the outing helped her keep proper perspective.

"A fool shows his annoyance at once, but a prudent man overlooks an insult." (Proverbs 12:1)

The second command is very difficult also.

2. "Whoever would love life and see good days must keep his tongue from evil and his lips from deceitful speech." (1 Peter 3:10)

For many women when they are in the war of abuse, the only weapon they have is their tongue. God says to control the tongue if you want to love life. With the tongue you are to respond to your husband with gentleness and respect. What an order from the Most High.

God always has good reasons for his command. Proverbs 15:1-2 gives two answers: You don't want to enrage your husband. Neither do you want to say foolish things in the heat of anger.

> A gentle answer turns away wrath, but a harsh word stirs up anger. (emphasis added) The tongue of the wise commands knowledge, but the mouth of the fool gushes folly.

When a husband is foolish, ugly, and repulsive, it is very difficult to want to honor him. The normal reaction is to tell him off, put him down, get even, or deceive him. Now if you honestly feel you don't have it in you to honor him, there is a way out. You can direct your respectful attitude to the office he holds as husband and father. Then when you feel better, you can respect him. Remember, pray to God. With His help you will persevere and enjoy life.

The third command is:

3. "... turn from evil and do good." (1 Peter 3:11a)

Another way to avoid abuse is to turn from evil and get away from it. When you feel you are losing control, go to another room or do an errand. Then ask yourself what you really want to accomplish. Proverbs 25:24 teaches a principle for avoiding a quarrelsome person. Here the husband goes to a corner of the roof to find peace. The roof in that instance would be like our porch. Perhaps you can find a "corner" where you can escape a husband who needles incessantly.

Lisa's voice rose in frustration. "Craig, I need some money to get the car fixed. After paying for Todd's braces, I don't have any money."

"I give you plenty of money to run this house," Craig retorted. "All you want is money, money, money."

Lisa's anger flared. "You didn't need that new pickup," she said. "You didn't consider the budget or our needs." She was losing control. She picked up the flowers she was arranging and carried them to the kitchen to get more water and get away. She wouldn't let Craig sidetrack her. He had no excuse not to give her money to fix the car. She needed to regain her composure and constructively and rationally confront him with their need. Her goal was to get money to have the car fixed, not to rehash and fight with him over the new pickup.

Then Lisa did something differently. <u>She reviewed carefully what Craig had said</u>. As she arranged her flowers quietly in the kitchen, his words came back to her.

"All you want is money, money, money."

It probably seemed that way. They had quarreled over the new pickup and money had often been an issue lately. How could she show Craig that money wasn't her main concern? She needed the car to meet the family's needs.

Lisa could think in this mode because that morning in her quiet time, God had reminded her she should return good for evil. She was also learning to listen to Craig—listen to learn what he really wanted. When she met his needs, he often met hers.

An idea popped into her head. She would write down all the reasons she needed the car next week. Then Craig could see her service to him in black and white.

If you are compassionate and respectful to your husband, he may listen to your ideas and concerns. When he does execute your idea, let him get the credit for it and give him praise for the outcome. If he goes against your wishes and makes a mistake, avoid gloating over his error. Treat him as a part of yourself and cheer him on. This can be very difficult to do when your man is proud and selfish and puts you down.

When you bless the wrongdoer, there is a promise. In fact, when you look on your trials as a "calling" from God, it is easier to bless the offender and the promise will be fulfilled—you will "inherit a blessing." (1 Peter 3:9) Claim the promise!

The fourth command is:

4. <u>Seek peace and pursue it</u>. (1 Peter 3:11b)

To seek peace and pursue it is an aggressive act. In the household of a difficult man sometimes the woman gives up and thinks letting him have complete control is the answer for peace. However, often times it works just the opposite. The more passive she becomes, the more obnoxious he becomes.

Darlene, a delightful Christian woman, had been married for fifteen years. To her dismay, her husband was getting worse every year. She submitted to his every whim to keep the peace. Passively, she complied to his sometimes ridiculous requests. Little did she realize she was losing his respect. She thought she was being a good Christian woman, but she was submerging her personality into a nonentity to keep the peace. To him, she became a boring drudge and he ran off with another woman. By not setting her standards and limits, she didn't help him be a better person and she also lost his interest.

To refuse to accept certain types of behavior is difficult to do in a godly manner. However, while your love for your spouse is patterned after God's love, which is unconditional, recognize that love is a living, active state. Acknowledging that you and your partner can destroy your emotional love for each other helps you set standards of behavior. These standards protect your love. When your spouse breaks them, let him know he is jeopardizing the love state in the family. But this must be done respectfully, graciously, and gently.

Take the most objectionable problem and let him know your standards. Be sure they follow God's Word.

"Putting me down all the time does not honor you or me. I will wait until you stop."

"Screaming isn't going to work anymore. I refuse to listen to you until you are rational and reasonable."

Be firm and definite. Don't allow yourself to be drawn into an argument. Make the statement and back it up. If you say, "This is one time you can't intimidate me," look him in the eye and refuse to be bullied. Quietly say what you want to say or do what you want to do. Many women lose their rationale and make idle threats and a lot of noise, which accomplishes nothing. A husband usually senses when a woman means what she says. Teddy Roosevelt's quote, "Speak softly and carry a big stick," applies here.

Remember, every husband is different. Ask God for wisdom in handling your mate. Do not put yourself in danger. Understand that some men don't address their problems at work, but instead take their frustration out on you. When you stand up to them and they find they can't get away with it, they quit their abuse.

Sometimes a good sense of humor is the best approach to peace. Life can get very serious and a good laugh now and then makes the heart merry. Laugh away your troubles. See the absurdity in things. If your husband is outrageously awful, try laughing.

To Jeannie, her husband's fit was like a little boy's tantrum. She laughed and said, "You might as well through yourself on the floor and kick your heels."

After she laughed, he saw the absurdity in his behavior and slinked off to the next room ashamed.

Cultivate a sense of humor and a lighter touch. Overlook some cross words and cheer him up. Then find something you both can laugh about. Avoid patronizing, but encourage him to enjoy life.

It takes strength to pursue peace, but God will help you. He is the God of order and peace.

The fifth command is:

5. "<u>But even if you should suffer for what is right, you are blessed</u>." (1 Peter 3:14a)

No one wants to suffer for any reason, let alone for doing what's right. It isn't fair. Yet God tells you because of your ungodly husband you might suffer for being a good wife.

One of the secrets of being able to suffer for righteousness without rebelling is being able to see the whole picture. As a visionary, you've asked God for a godly home and for the salvation of your husband, and you are working toward that end. God tells you that <u>you are blessed</u>.

You are blessed for many reasons. Christ suffered and died for you that you might be saved. You are emulating Him in your suffering and that pleases Christ. You are also blessed because there is a condition with the hope of your husband's salvation. You are meeting that condition by your obedience. No matter what your husband's behavior is, you are meeting the condition by your faith. This means you can have great hope in asking God for your husband's salvation. It will be fulfilled in God's good time if He so desires.

When you suffer for any reason, there are problems. Well-meaning but glib people say, "Thank God for your trials." This may be correct, but sometimes you need time to work into such an attitude. God understands this. In Lamentations 3 He lets His servant Jeremiah express his grief and frustration. "He has besieged me and surrounded me with bitterness and hardship. (Lamentations 3:5)

But though Jeremiah lamented for his trials and sins, he saw the hand of God in all his suffering. This enabled him to examine himself further, confess and go forward with hope for he believed God is good. Depending on God's character, he then could have a hopeful and positive attitude.

God's way goes against all worldly wisdom. It is hard and sometimes it requires sacrifice and humility. God's way sometimes makes no sense. But it will in time.

George MacDonald, that Scottish novelist of old, said, "Had he done as the Master told him, he would soon have come to understand. Obedience is the opener of eyes." (George MacDonald, C. S. Lewis 61 Knowledge, p. 28)

James 1:2 says, "Consider it joy, my brothers, whenever you face trials of many kinds, because you know that the testing of your faith develops perseverance."

You find Christian maturity among many spiritually widowed wives for they have obeyed and persevered. Perhaps that is part of the blessing.

The sixth command is:

6. "Keeping a clear conscience." (1 Peter 3:16b)

When you have a clear conscience you are free. No one can honestly say anything bad about your faith or your life. Christ is honored. There is joy in life no matter the circumstance.

But when you are under siege in a poor marriage, you often fail. Then your conscience whips up shame, depression, anger and hatred toward your partner.

What can you do to keep a clear conscience? First you realize that you probably will fail at one time or another. Be prepared. Consider yourself in a stormy sea. A monstrous wave boils over the side of the boat knocking you down on the deck. You cling to the mast until the wave subsides and then you get up and bail water. Sometimes you work like fury to keep the boat afloat. You are in a survival situation.

So, too, a woman married to an angry, unhappy man must struggle to survive. Big waves of sin will knock you down. As you cling to the mast—Jesus Christ—you will be stabilized. Then you bail out the sin which threatens to sink you. Don't give up. Don't collapse, but hang in there. Soon there will be a breather. Keep a clear conscience by confessing your sin and receiving forgiveness.

PRACTICAL GUIDES FOR DEALING WITH A DIFFICULT MATE

1. Confess your sins to God and accept forgiveness. If needed, ask your husband for forgiveness. Forgive your husband when he seeks it or cover sins in love.

2. Take time to be objective. Back off. Remember, your partner has irrational behavior and thinking when he loses control. Don't allow him to drag you down into his irrational ways.

3. Get away for a break. It is important to have times of refreshment. Often the encouragement and inspiration of a Bible study is all you need. If your family doesn't live close by, plan a vacation to see them if it is at all possible. Maybe they will help in the expense of travel. Admit your troubles and don't be too proud to accept help. If they live close by, maybe your parents or

siblings will plan a fun time for you and your children for a weekend. A trip to the zoo and a visit to their church may be all you need. If you don't have family that will help, maybe someone in your church can be "substitute parents."

4. Avoid depression. Share everything with God. Pray for a friend who will be a good support and in whom you can <u>confide and trust</u>.

5. Don't badger yourself with guilt. Expect failure at times, but learn to quickly pick yourself up and continue on your way.

6. Find some release—an art class, gardening, job, hobby, something you enjoy doing so much you lose yourself and forget your problems.

7. Don't be surprised when other people don't understand. Expect criticism but don't internalize it into guilt.

8. Try to protect your children from being drawn into arguments and trouble. However, don't keep them in the dark, but have them pray for your family. Teach them to love their father.

9. Say often the old saying, "As you will, Lord. This, too, will pass…"

10. Look forward to better days and God's blessings.

TROUBLED SOUL

Troubled soul, you are not required to feel but you are required to rise up. God loves you whether you feel it or not. Maybe you can't love when you will, but you are bound to fight the hatred in you to the last. Try not to feel good when you aren't good, but cry to Him who is good. He doesn't change because you change. No, He has a special tenderness of love toward you for you are in the dark and have no light, and His heart is glad when you get up and say, "I will go to my Father." ... Fold your arms of faith and wait in the quietness until light begins to shine in your darkness.

In faith and not depending on your own will power, think of something you should do, and go do it, if it is only sweeping a room, or preparing a meal, or visiting a friend. Don't consider your feeling: do your work. (George MacDonald, 365 Readings, collected by C. S. Lewis, paraphrased by Rosemarie Malroy)

CHAPTER NINE

BIBLE STUDY AND DISCUSSION

Read the Scripture and discuss each verse. Can you apply it to your life?

Finally, all of you, live in harmony with one another; be sympathetic, love as brothers, be compassionate and humble. 9 Do not repay evil with evil or insult with insult, but with blessing, because, to this you were called so that you may inherit a blessing. 10 For,

"Whoever would love life
and see good days
must keep his tongue from evil
and his lips from deceitful speech.
11 He must turn from evil and do good;
he must seek peace and pursue it.
12 For the eyes of the Lord are on the righteous
and his ears are attentive to their prayer,
but the face of the Lord is against those who do evil."

13 Who is going to harm you if you are eager to do good?
14 But even if you should suffer for what is right, you are
blessed. "Do not fear what they fear, do not be frightened."
15 But in your hearts set apart Christ as Lord. Always be
prepared to give an answer to everyone who asks you to
give the reason for the hope that you have. 16 But do this
with gentleness and respect, keeping a clear conscience, so
that those who speak maliciously against your good
behavior in Christ may be ashamed of their slander. 17 It is
better, if it is God's will, to suffer for doing good than for
doing evil (1 Peter 3:8-17)

CHAPTER NINE QUESTIONS

1. If we don't repay evil for evil or insult with insult, what promise do we have?

   _____

   _____

   _____

2. What comfort do you find in verse 12? (1 Peter 3:12)

   _____

   _____

3. Why should we be willing to suffer for doing good?

   _____

   _____

4. Describe a home where there is a possibility that the husband will ask the wife about her faith.

   _____

   _____

5. How are you supposed to witness to those who ask you questions about your faith?

   _____

   _____

6. In countries (China, Russia, Eritrea in Africa, etc.) where Christians have suffered for doing right—some with their own lives—Christianity has doubled. Why do you think this has happened?

_____

_____

Rosemarie D. Malroy

Chapter Ten
DECIDING TO STAY OR LEAVE

The question needs to be asked, "Why would God ever require a woman to stay with a husband who is unkind, unloving, and sometimes cruel?

In the magazine <u>Tabletalk</u> author Terry Johnson asks another question: "Has the liberalizing of divorce laws in the last several decades resulted in a net decrease in human suffering or a net increase?" Herein holds the answer to God's tough stand in the Scriptures concerning divorce.

When the Pharisees questioned Jesus about divorce, Jesus referred back to the creation ordinance of marriage and said, "Therefore what God has joined together, let not man separate." (Matthew 19:6b) That is the rule— that is God's standard. The only exceptions to the rule in Scripture are unrepentant sexual immorality (Matthew 19:9) and desertion (1 Corinthians 7:15).

God is tough but that doesn't mean He doesn't care for you and your suffering. He sees the broader picture. He knows that the ultimate happiness of a people lies in their high view of marriage; not in some idealized dream, but in the covenant or contract of marriage. When that contract is broken, the impact on society as a whole is great. Men, women, and children suffer as families are broken and divorce and remarriage continue until children's children are so confused they don't know what constitutes a family. The

115

bedrock of society is jarred loose sending everyone in a spin looking futilely for happiness. Broken people on every side cry out for love. Yes, God cares. He cares so much that He makes tough laws, so we will shape up and find happiness.

"Wait a minute," you say. "How about me? I've tried my best. You don't know the suffering I've gone through. Doesn't God care about me?"

Let's get back to you. You are very precious to Him. He does care. He wants the very best for you, so let's investigate further whether you should stay or leave.

Catherine's husband was controlling and demanding. He owned his own business and expected Catherine to do the bookwork and janitorial service for the business offices. He also expected her to keep up the house, cook economical and delicious meals, and entertain guests. Catherine had very little money to call her own and no time for herself. He got so ugly when she went to church, she finally went spasmodically—when she had the strength to go against his iron will.

One day she couldn't take it any longer.

"I cracked up," she said. "My youngest son was still in high school and wanted to stay home with his dad, but I felt I had to leave. With no money and nowhere to go, I took off and found a job as a bookkeeper. I did make it on my own, but one night before the divorce was final, I lay in bed crying and reading my Bible when a verse hit me between the eyes. "A wife must not separate from her husband. But if she does she must remain unmarried or else be reconciled to her husband. And a husband must not divorce his wife." (1 Corinthians 7:10b-11)

"It was as if God in all His holiness spoke out loud to me. According to that verse, I was wrong to leave and if I separated, I couldn't remarry and I wasn't to divorce. How could I live like that? I couldn't. I didn't have it in me."

"Picking up the phone, I did the hardest thing I ever did in my life. I asked my husband to take me back, but I told him I would like him to agree on certain issues. I needed to go to church and have freedom to have some time to myself with a little spending money I could call my own. To my surprise, he welcomed me home."

Catherine has been married over fifty years now and her children rise up and call her blessed. Her husband is still difficult and not a Christian, but he takes her on fun vacations all over the world. She's still praying for him with faith and hope.

"I'm grateful that through His Word, God intervened and kept my family intact. Now grandchildren fill our home and though my husband is not a Christian, we are teaching our family by example about the sanctity of marriage." God helped Catherine to make a wise decision and He will help you too.

Darby, a homemaker and fragile young mother of three, was determined to have a Christian family even though at present her husband wasn't a Christian. She could do it! All she needed was faith. Then her husband began a downward spiral using alcohol and drugs. At first he left for just a night at a time, but then it lengthened into days and finally weeks. When he came home, he was hateful.

Then he started beating Darby and humiliating her in front of their children. Her pastor and friends tried to convince her that she should separate. She, however, determined he was going to be a Christian and all she needed was faith and love. For two years she begged him to stay home, enduring his abuse.

Finally, one day when he came home and she begged him to stay, he turned to her and said, "Can't you see, I don't want you."

Broken-hearted Darby came to realize that's what he had been telling her all along. "But if the unbelieving depart, let him depart." (1 Corinthians 7:15) <u>The first time he hit her, she should have left the house and gotten help to address the problem.</u> Then if he had wanted to participate in the marriage, he would have gone for counseling with her.

God did bless Darby's faith and love in another way. Two years later found her happily married with a man who was a godly husband and a wonderful father to her children.

There are certain times when a woman should leave. If you are a battered woman, separate. Lois Hoadley Dick in her article "The Unheard Screams of Private Violence" defines battering as premeditated, deliberate, terrorism from a man who has low self-esteem and has usually grown up seeing a parent abused. Often the battered woman is an emotionally and economically dependent woman who grew up seeing her mother mistreated. Violence can be verbal as well as physical.

In his article "Leading Victims to Victory," Ronald E. Hawkins says,

> The greatest way she [the wife] can show her love for her abusive husband is to make him accountable, pray for him, and set in motion a process that could result in his change. Almost without exception this will involve the intervention of the courts. They alone possess the power to mandate change in the abusive system and monitor accountability. This will be important since initially the only thing the abuser fears is a power greater than his own. If he is not mandated by the court for counseling, he will simply move on into another abusive situation. Another woman, other children, will become his victims. Tough love may result in his change and the ultimate salvation of the entire family from a cycle of violence.

Chief Bouza as early as 1983 in the <u>Parade Magazine</u> said, "Arrest appears to be the best way of deterring domestic violence." These were the results of the pioneering 16-month study of the Minneapolis Police Department. Today the results are the same.

Beverly, after the death of her husband, met a man at church. "He kindly helped me with many problems," she said. "Letting him take over and relaxing a bit from the stress and strain of the past year was wonderful." Soon they married, but Beverly's happiness degenerated into the control of an abusive man.

Tim Kimmel, in his article "Living with a Controller," explains that in a good marriage both dependence (need to be needed) and independence (privacy or space) need to be included. Beverly's husband gradually took away all her space and freedom to be an individual. Hurt and frustrated, Beverly reacted with angry words.

"That was when the big bang came," she said. Her husband socked her in the eye and sent her whirling. Beverly was a battered woman.

Confused and guilty because of her hot tongue, she excused her new husband. He, too, seemed very remorseful and apologized. But once the cycle started, it continued. Finally the escalating of the violence caused her to realize her serious situation. Then she found she wasn't the first woman he had battered.

Beverly left and got a restraining order. She was fortunate in that she had not slipped into the addictive mode of the battered wife.

Maxine V. Hoffman's experience with battered women helped her describe the pattern to all battering incidents in a cycle of three phases.

1. The first phase involves the build-up of tension between the couple. Verbal fighting often occurs here. Sometimes the wife in fear tries to please her husband and complies with his every wish. (Can last from several days to years.)

2. The second phase of the cycle is the explosion of the husband's rage where he beats her to discipline her. (Lasts usually from 2 to 24 hours.)

3. In the third phase they make up. The husband asks forgiveness and gives promises and gifts. Sometimes the wife, in order to excuse his behavior, rationalizes that maybe she really does deserve his anger. And then the cycle starts over.

Hoffman says, "Throughout the cycle such wives constantly suppress two emotions: the overwhelming fear that they might be killed, and rage that they have absolutely no control over the situation."

Fear and rage both can be crippling emotions. In 1 Peter 3:14b God commands,

"Do not fear what they fear, do not be frightened."

How can a woman who lives in the terror of possible eruption of a raging wife beater not fear? With God's help she takes action. She plans her way of escape. This decision is not based on pride, hurt, or justice, but on her safety, mental well-being and health, and that of her children.

BATTERED WIVES

- Battering occurs in all age, economic, educational and racial groups

- Most all wife beaters were beaten during their childhood or saw their mothers beaten.

- Battering husbands are not necessarily violent people to start with.

- The cause of the batter's anger comes from feelings of worthlessness, frustration and extreme tension from the work force and rage against society.

- Women stay in such relationships because they feel helpless, worthless, and unable to cope.

- Many battered women love their husbands.

- A wife beater often isolates and controls his wife because he fears losing her—the only person who makes him feel powerful.

- Battered wives don't enjoy such treatment!

PLANNING A WAY OF ESCAPE

1. Find a helper who will listen to your story of abuse without shock or judgment. It may be your pastor, a mature woman at church, a Christian friend, or family member.

2. Find a helper who is knowledgeable enough to know that battered woman do not "deserve" or "need" to be battered, nor do they "ask for it."

3. Have them help you locate the necessary help you need, whatever it might be—

   • Free legal aid

   • Counseling for you and your mate

   • A place to stay

   • Child care

   • A job

4. Pray to the Lord for guidance and wisdom to proceed, and then do your part.

5. Take action for the benefit of your husband, children, and yourself.

6. Remember, "The greatest way you can show your love to your abusive husband is to make him accountable for his actions and set in motion a process that could result in his change."

7. After leaving him, do not go back unless he submits to counseling and has complied with their recommendations. (Be sure to get competent counseling—ask your pastor.)

8. If your husband expresses any attempt to violence because of your actions, call 911 and have him arrested.

9. Be sure to take with you any legal papers you might need. (Birth certificates, house deed, school records, check book, etc.)

Do not back down. You need the legal system to help you. If his abuse continues, ask for a restraining order. If that doesn't work, have a permanent restraining order or ask for imprisonment. When he continues in behavior that he knows will result in forced separation, he may be regarded as willfully deserting his spouse. Go to your church. Let them counsel you and help you with a divorce.

It never pays to hide abuse. Alison was so ashamed when Michael started slapping her around that she told no one. *It only happens when he is really upset about something*, she rationalized to herself. One day friends accidentally witnessed his abuse. When the word got around to friends, family, and church members, they wisely put social pressure on Michael to reform. Ashamed, he stopped such action. They nipped such behavior in the bud. Social action against battering can be very helpful. A woman should not hide physical abuse.

Knowing when to stay or leave is not always cut and dry. Sometimes you make mistakes. Sometimes even when it isn't physical abuse, you feel you can't stand another minute of it.

"I understand how you feel," Lisa told some friends who were discouraged. "We shouldn't talk badly about our husbands, but this happened years ago and maybe it will help see that things do change. I tried to leave when the children were very small. I remember it vividly. The baby had colic all morning and then the phone rang. It was Craig.

'I'm bringing a client home for dinner. Be ready this time,' he said.

'Craig, I'm tired. I don't feel like' … bang! He had slammed the phone down on me. There was a house to clean and a dinner to make in a few hours and the baby was crying again.

Behind schedule, I stooped over the sink peeling potatoes when he came stomping in the house.

'What? You're just peeling potatoes? He's going to be here in thirty minutes.' He stormed to the refrigerator, grabbed a drink, and set it on the coffee table. Throwing his business papers down, he jerked off his tie and threw down his jacket on the couch. Then he took his shower. By the time he got out our son had tipped over his drink and I was frantically trying to clean it up.

'This house is a mess,' he screamed. 'Joe is an important client.'

'You made this mess,' I screamed back."

"Wait a minute," Dana interrupted the story. "I want to know why you were so stupid to ever have a client for dinner."

"Yeah," laughed Jan.

"Well" Lisa explained. "Craig and I had an agreement. I'd have them for dinner if he wouldn't entertain them at a bar."

"Oh, I see—go ahead with your story."

"The dinner was over," Lisa continued. "I was seething and Craig was angry. He got up and said, 'Joe and I are going to the bar for a few drinks.'

After he left, I started to cry. 'I'm getting a divorce,' I said, meaning it. I grabbed some suitcases and piled them full of baby clothes, kid clothes, and my clothes. I wasn't going to take his abuse any longer. Grabbing the kids, I hurried out of the house. He had moved our car out in the yard to get his truck out.

Darkness fell silently on our home. The light from the porch was just a circle of white leaving the car in shadows. Angrily, I backed up the car … CLUNK … The car wouldn't budge. I revved the motor and the tires spun. Getting out I found I was hung up on a stump.

'God,' I cried. 'I can't even run away. Even Jonah got further.'"

"You hung in there," Jan said laughing. Once I left too. I left for less reason than you did. I thought my husband boring, selfish, and noncommunicative. The Scripture that corrected me was Matthew 5:43-48:

> You have heard that it was said, "Love your neighbor and hate your enemy." But I tell you: Love your enemies and pray for those who persecute you that you may be sons of your Father in heaven. He causes his sun to rise on the evil and the good, and sends rain on the righteous and the unrighteous. If you love those who love you, what reward will you get? Are not even the tax collectors doing that? And if you greet only your brother, what are you doing more than others? Do not even pagans do that? Be perfect, therefore, as your heavenly Father is perfect.

"It said we are to love our enemies. I didn't consider my husband my enemy. I just couldn't stand him. God showed me I'd better start loving him."

She turned to Lisa and asked, "Lisa, what are some principles that help you when things get hard?

Lisa thought carefully. "One thing I've learned is that the only person I have to please is God. If I please Him, all else will work out. Sometimes I feel I'm pulled in a hundred directions and sometimes Craig puts hard demands on me, but God is the one I answer to ultimately.

Then if my passion is God's good name—revealing that He is good, my suffering is secondary. It makes suffering easier because my joy is found in God, not in my circumstances.

It also helps to understand that some things are hard. I haven't failed or done anything wrong. I just need to "hang in there." God will help. And then, of course, Craig and I have good times together. It's easy to concentrate on the bad times and forget all the good times. He is a talented man, and we have a beautiful home. Even though he is sometimes difficult I know he loves us. I am thankful."

The bottom line of whether a woman should stay or leave is not her happiness. In marriage there are good times and bad. The frustrations of today become inconsequential in view of a lifetime and future generations. As one thrice-married woman told her frustrated and unhappy daughter-in-law, "Dear, you just trade one set of problems for another when you change partners."

Ultimately each woman has to make the decision herself whether to separate or stay with her husband. She alone has to answer to God, her spouse, her children, and future generations. The widowed wife needs to obey God and ask for wisdom and good biblical counselors to help her know whether she should stay or leave.

Keep your lives free from the love of money and be content with what you have, because God has said, "Never will I leave you; never will I forsake you." So we say with confidence, "The Lord is my helper; I will not be afraid. What can man do to me?" (Hebrews 13:5-6)

Targeting Unhappiness

1. Count your blessings.
2. Enjoy blessings.
3. See the whole picture.
4. Quit dwelling on unhappiness.

CHAPTER TEN
BIBLE STUDY AND DISCUSSION

Should I Stay or Leave?

STAY

The man said, "This is now bone of my bones and flesh of my flesh; she shall be called 'woman,' for she was taken out of man." For this reason a man will leave his father and mother and be united to his wife, and they will become one flesh. (Genesis 2:23 & 24)

But I tell you that anyone who divorces his wife, except for marital unfaithfulness, causes her to commit adultery, and anyone who marries a woman so divorced commits adultery. (Matthew 5:32)

To the married I give this command (not I but the Lord): A wife must not separate from her husband. 11 But if she does, she must remain unmarried or else be reconciled to her husband. And a husband must not divorce his wife. 12 To the rest I say this (I, not the Lord): If any brother has a wife who is not a believer and she is willing to live with him, he must not divorce her. 13 And a woman has a husband who is not a believer and he is willing to live with her, she must not divorce him. 14 For the unbelieving husband has been sanctified through his wife, and the unbelieving wife has been sanctified through her believing husband. Otherwise your children would be unclean, but as it is, they are holy. (1 Corinthians 7:10-14)

Therefore what God has joined together, let man not separate." (Mark 10:9)

For example, by law a married woman is bound to her husband as long as he is alive, but if her husband dies, she is released from the law of marriage. (Romans 7:2)

LEAVE

But if the unbeliever leaves, let him do so. A believing man or woman is not bound in such circumstances; God has called us to live in peace. 16 How do you know, wife, whether you will save your husband? Or, how do you know, husband, whether you will save your wife? (1 Corinthians 7: 15-16)

I tell you that anyone who divorces his wife, except for marital unfaithfulness, and marries another woman commits adultery. (Matthew 19:9)

You shall not murder (Safety of you and your family). (Exodus 20:13)

But if she does, she must remain unmarried or else be reconciled to her husband. (1 Corinthians 7:11)

CHAPTER TEN QUESTIONS

"How do you know, wife, whether you will save your husband?" (1 Corinthians 7:16a)

1. God emphasizes that He considers a man and wife to be one flesh by repeating this Scripture in the New Testament. Why does He consider them one unit not to be broken?

   _____

   _____

2. What exception for divorce does He give in Matthew 19:9?

   _____

   _____

3. What reason does God's word give for allowing a Christian to divorce a non-Christian when the non-Christian wants to leave?

   _____

   _____

4. When a Christian wants to leave because she is tired of being married to a non-Christian, should she do so? Why or why not?

   _____

   _____

5. If a woman has an opportunity to marry a much better man, should she do so? Why or why not?

_____

_____

6. What Scripture is behind the reason a woman should leave a wife beater? (See Exodus 20:13)

_____

_____

7. Our society treats marriage very lightly. Explain why you think the Creator does not.

_____

_____

REASONS TO STAY OR LEAVE

Stay	Leave
1. _____	1. _____
2. _____	2. _____
3. _____	3. _____
4. _____	4. _____
5. _____	5. _____
6. _____	6. _____

Rosemarie D. Malroy

RAIN

Rain,
dripping, slipping,
gliding, sliding
down the window pane.

I see it now
on branch and bough,
a soft and gentle
rain.

A leaf upturned,
dainty cup,
sags beneath
its weight,

Then spills its contents
to the ground,
its burden
much too great.

God
sheds His mercies,
like the rain,
in soft and gentle flow,

Upon His children
in their pain,
His love
to freely show.

And we,
like fragile vessels, too,
need daily
to release

Our burdens
and our cares to Him
to find
His promised peace.

Shirley S. Miller
7/26/92 & 2/3/93

Chapter Eleven
LOVING THE UNLOVELY

Mrs. Turner, a little old lady with sterling hair, served Lisa tea in Spode china. Her husband's conversion after fifty years of marriage was the talk of the church. Lisa had come to ask this humble woman a question. She waited for the right moment, hoping the words were well chosen.

"What is the most important thing you did to prepare the way for your husband to become a Christian?" she asked.

Mrs. Turner looked at Lisa kindly. "Why loving him," she exclaimed. "Loving him up one side and down the other," she said chuckling. "That's the most important thing."

Lisa murmured a quiet little "Oh." She didn't tell Mrs. Turner how dejected that made her feel. Maybe Mr. Turner hadn't been as difficult as Craig. Why didn't the older lady say she prayed for him or she trusted in God? That would be easier. Was God highlighting her weakest point—her inability to love the unlovely? Craig wasn't always unlovely. When he was, Lisa's heart clamped down and snapped shut.

How do you love the unlovely? The following seven points helped Lisa, and hopefully you, too, will benefit from them.

1. Change Thyself—With God's Help

M. Basilea Schlink in her book <u>The Hidden Treasure in Suffering</u> tells how she learned to love the unlovely. God used some difficult circumstances to teach her to love God's way.

She lived with a person whose selfishness, envy, and rebellion surfaced in irrational accusations and fits of rage. She made life unbearable. No matter how Basilea tried to keep peace, it didn't work. Bitterness walled them both into their cubbyholes of misery. Basilea could see no way to communicate or hope for a restored relationship. Others agreed with her. Tired of trying she desperately prayed to God for help.

"You are the one who has to change," God told her.

> Where is your love for your closest neighbor? (Matthew 5:43-44) You hide resentment and bitter thoughts in your heart. (Hebrews 12:15) <u>But if you do not forgive men their sins,</u> your Father will not forgive your sins." (Matthew 6:15, emphasis added)

Broken and convicted of her sins, Basilea prayed for a contrite heart. Every morning for twenty minutes she prayed for true repentance for her bitterness. Months passed. Then God answered her prayer. He took away her bitterness and gave her a forgiving heart. Now she had a genuine love for her roommate even though her roommate hadn't changed.

One day her companion erupted in an angry tirade. This time Basilea reacted in a completely different way. Instead of closing her heart in defense, she felt love welling up. She took her roommate and tenderly kissed her on the cheek. That person stopped in astonishment. Basilea knew it was the time to ask forgiveness for her bitter feelings. When she did, it opened her companion's heart. She never was the same again. Gradually, God worked until she, too, was transformed.

Two women transformed because one woman took God's Word seriously. She patterned her love after Christ's love.

"<u>While we were still sinners, Christ died for us</u>." (Romans 5:8b, emphasis added)

Like Christ, Basilea stepped out and loved one who was scarred and malformed in personality and heart. She took Christ's love and let it flow through her to the unlovely one. God abundantly blessed. By suffering daily with a difficult person, she was changed to be more Christlike and the love changed her companion. With God's help you, too, can change and love the unlovely.

2. Act in Love

Basilea had bitter feelings when she came to God—there was no love for her roommate. Yet she acted. She acted out love by praying for a better heart. Christ defines love by saying,

"<u>Do to others what you would have them do to you</u>." (Matthew 7:12, emphasis added)

Love is action oriented. You love your husband when you do what is best for him—in spite of your feelings.

3. Fan the Flames of Love

In George MacDonald's reading, "What Cannot Be Loved," he suggests fanning the flame of that little bit of fading good in the unlovely one. Instead of concentrating on all the black smudges of sin, try to find some lovableness and concentrate on it. Focus on that spark of trust you may have for that person. Look for those things you want to see. Be positive. Don't look for the ugliness you expect to see. Be bright. Hope for happiness. Plan for success. Direct yourself the way you want to go. Expect to retrieve confident trust, innocent acceptance, and gentle closeness. Depend on God.

4. Fall in Love Again

When you change, your mate will see a positive, success-oriented wife who accepts him even if you don't accept all his actions. This helps him respond positively. Instead of alienating him, you draw him to your side. Then the emotions of love can take over. You can fell in love again and that gentle closeness will be a wonderful part of your life.

Of course, there will be hard times, but the good will compensate. Then you can enlarge your focus and spend more time developing yourself and serving others. You will be free to be you—not always dragged down in the pit.

5. Love Depends on You

To grow in grace is necessary in order to love the unlovely. Why?

Because God's love and our Christian love is not based on the worth of the loved one, but on the character of the one who loves.

You must be lovely to love the unlovely. Go to God every day for strength, wisdom, and cleansing.

6. Develop Self-sufficient Love

You cannot expect any person you love to meet all your needs. Because of your love for your husband, you learn to be independent. Fill in for your loved one. Instead of rejecting him because he isn't giving you what you want, be creative and provide for your own needs. Focus on meeting his.

Suzanne's work isolated her all day. When her husband came home, she needed and expected him to talk with her. Instead, he ignored her and looked at TV. When she complained, he said, "Be quiet. I'm looking at the news." Hurt, she retreated into her protective shell. Gradually a silent wall rose between them. A desire not met was tearing the marriage apart. It made a very unhappy Suzanne. She focused more on her loneliness and unwittingly rejected her husband.

A housebound friend came to her rescue. "Give me a call when you get home. I'm alone all day with the kids." Suzanne learned to meet her own social needs by interacting with her friend. She redirected her focus and this enabled her to accept her uncommunicative husband. She also found because she let her husband rest after work and he didn't feel pressured to talk, later conversation flowed more freely.

God always loves us even though we ignore Him. We try to pattern our love after God's love. A stable love stands alone not depending on what it gets. It is self-sufficient.

7. See as God Sees

Lisa learned it was possible to love a difficult person if she could see him through God's eyes … see him as a needy sinner like us all. One of Lisa's problems was that she compared her husband to Christian men. "He fell short," she said. "I didn't want to love a person who makes me ashamed. I guess part of my problem is pride. When I remember I am a needy sinner like Craig, it is easier to love him. I never seem to learn this completely," Lisa said, "but I am trying."

Loving the unlovely is no easy task. Yet in the end if you help retrieve a wandering sheep, it will be well worth it. Even if that is not the end result, if you follow God's way of love, you will be beautiful.

C. S. Lewis, in his book The Four Loves, explains we need God's help to love the unlovely. The ability to love another with a selfless love is a gift given to us by God. He says, "But Divine Gift-love in the man enables him to love what is not naturally lovable; lepers, criminals, enemies, morons, the

sulky, the superior and the sneering."

CHAPTER ELEVEN
BIBLE STUDY AND DISCUSSION

Read the Scripture and discuss each verse. How can you apply these commands of Christ to your life?

> You have heard that it was said, "Love your neighbor and hate your enemy." 44 But I tell you: Love your enemies and pray for those who persecute you, 45 that you may be sons of your Father in heaven. He causes his sun to rise on the evil and the good, and sends rain on the righteous and the unrighteous. 46 If you love those who love you, what reward will you get? Are not even the tax collectors doing that? 47 And if you greet only your brothers, what are you doing more than others? Do not even pagans do that? 48 Be perfect, therefore, as your heavenly Father is perfect (Matthew 5:43-48)

CHAPTER ELEVEN QUESTIONS

1. Why are we supposed to love our enemies?

   _____

   _____

2. What does God command us to do for our enemies?

   _____

   _____

3. What does God say when we are loving to our husbands when they are good to us, but hateful to them when they aren't nice?

_____

_____

4. What is the reason we are to love the unlovely?

    _____

    _____

5. Why does God command us to be perfect?

    _____

    _____

6. Do you think He might be reminding us of our imperfections so we won't be harsh on others?

    _____

    _____

7. How can we be loving to someone when we don't have a forgiving spirit?

    _____

    _____

Rosemarie D. Malroy

Chapter Twelve
YOUR UNIQUE HUSBAND

Men have basic needs that often are mysteries to women. The basic need of all men is to be loved. The emphasis of their love need might be a little different than women.

They want to be:

- Trusted

- Accepted

- Appreciated

- Admired

- Approved

- Encouraged

Bonnie responded bitterly to this list. "How can I trust my husband when he isn't trustworthy, or admire him when I don't approve of his actions?" she asked.

Bonnie had a valid complaint. Her husband treated her in a very unloving way after she became a Christian. He seemed to be doing everything to reject her. He broke her trust, was unkind, and seemed to delight in doing things she didn't approve of any more. What could she do?

The Bible has the answer. First Corinthians 13:4-7 tells us how to love. Love:

- Is patient
- Is kind
- Does not envy
- Does not boast
- Is not proud
- Is not rude
- Is not self-seeking
- Is not easily angered
- Keeps no record of wrongs
- Does not delight in evil
- Rejoices with the truth
- Always protects
- Always trusts
- Always hopes
- Always perseveres

Bonnie unintentionally made her husband feel very unloved. She was impatient because of his ungodly ways. She felt ashamed of him and he sensed it. She exhibited pride. When she tried to change his ways and he rejected her efforts, she grew cold and aloof and felt very superior to him.

She punished him by pouting and fighting. That turned into a rude scene. She manipulated him by trying to make him feel guilty. She grew very angry when he didn't respond to her wishes and brooded over the wrongs he did to her. She called her friends and told them of his misdeeds and how awful he behaved. He knew when she was talking about him, even though he didn't say anything. She did not trust him after he deceived her, and she had given up hope. She wanted to quit.

It is easy for any woman to react like Bonnie. When you hurt inside, the tendency is to lash out, not love. When your mate makes you ashamed or unloved, <u>you</u> want to change him. But God says that isn't love.

What could Bonnie do to improve her relationship with her husband? How could she best express love to him when she felt so unloved? Bonnie could do a very simple thing. <u>She could exercise her love by not trying to change him or improve him</u>. To do this, she shouldn't punish him when he disappointed her. If she held her tongue and didn't try to get even, then he would feel accepted. To be accepted helps men feel loved.

Bonnie tried doing things God's way. She trusted God to change her husband. Then she relaxed and surrendered or submitted to her husband in that she didn't try to change him. She put her energies into having a forgiving spirit. She worked on her own happiness, so she did not depend on him to make her happy. She also tried to show appreciation when he provided for her needs. This made him feel needed. She also praised him for the good things he did.

Any man wants to be loved. When a woman does not try to improve him, he feels accepted and loved. This will help him grow more than anything you can do, and it paves the way so he will listen when you confront him concerning serious matters.

ASSIGNMENT

1. Next week try to go a whole week without criticizing your husband in any way. Don't use put-downs by expression or inference.

2. Express your wishes, but don't make him feel you are trying to change him. You may say, "I feel upset when you curse the kids" or "Please don't curse the kids." Then leave it at that, letting him know it is up to him to change. Don't try to "get even" for his bad actions.

3. When he hurts you, concentrate on a forgiving attitude instead of nurturing the hurt.

4. Figure out ways to make yourself happy. Sometimes reading a good novel can get you away from your own problems. Then you can be more objective.

5. Read 1 Corinthians 13 every day.

Every woman has to work at inspiring her husband to grow as an individual. God's way is always the best way. Let God do the changing and you concentrate on the loving. With God's help you can do all things.

* * *

Your husband is unique. To complement him means making changes. This may often lead to delightful surprises. Helen was a city girl. She fell in love and married a young man whose work took them to the countryside. She found she had to adjust to another style of living. At first it was hard, but when she allowed herself to enjoy some of the wonderful things about country living, she adapted very well. There is no growth when your mind closes. God puts you in new situations so you can spread your wings and fly—often in a different direction than you ever imagined.

CHAPTER TWELVE

BIBLE STUDY AND DISCUSSION

Read the Scripture and discuss each verse. How can you practically use this wisdom to love your husband?

> If I speak in the tongues of men and angels, but have not love, I am only a resounding gong or a clanging cymbal. 2 If I have the gift of prophecy and can fathom all mysteries and all knowledge, and if I have a faith that can move mountains, but have not love, I am nothing. 3 If I give all I possess to the poor and surrender my body to the flames, but have not love, I gain nothing.
>
> Love is patient, love is kind. It does not envy, it does not boast, it is not proud.
>
> 5 It is not rude, it is not self-seeking, it is not easily angered, it keeps no record of wrongs. 6 Love does not delight in evil but rejoices with the truth. 7 It always protects, always trusts, always hopes, always perseveres.
>
> Love never fails. But where there are prophecies, they will cease; where there are tongues, they will be stilled; where there is knowledge, it will pass away. 9 For we know in part and we prophesy in part, 10 but when perfection comes, the imperfect disappears. 11 When I was a child, I talked like a child, I thought like a child, I reasoned like a child. When I became a man, I put childish ways behind me. 12 Now we see but a poor reflection; then we shall see face to face. Now I know in part; then I shall know fully, even as I am fully known.
>
> And now these three remain: faith, hope and love. But the greatest of these is love. (1 Corinthians 13)

A GIFT OF LOVE TO MY HUSBAND

by Bonnie

I will trust him to overcome his bitterness because I became a Christian.

I will accept him by not criticizing him or trying to change him.

I will appreciate him by remembering the good he does instead of the bad.

I will admire the characteristics that attracted him to me in the first place.

I will encourage him by letting him know he is needed.

   1. I will trust

   _____

   _____

   2. I will accept

   _____

   _____

   3. I will appreciate

   _____

   _____

   4. I will admire

   _____

   _____

CHAPTER TWELVE QUESTIONS

1. Name three ways a Christian can show patience to her non-Christian husband.

   a. _____

   b. _____

   c. _____

2. How can envy be expressed by a spiritually widowed wife?

   _____

   _____

   _____

3. How can boasting about your troubles happen? (My troubles are worse than yours.)

   _____

   _____

   _____

4. How can a spiritually widowed wife be proud?

   _____

   _____

5. It is popular on TV shows to be rude. Define rude.

   _____

   _____

6. Give an example of how a wife can be rude to her husband.

    _____

    _____

7. How can a wife be self-seeking?

    _____

8. If she is so ambitious she neglects her family, is she self-seeking? Why or why not?

    _____

    _____

9. A woman sometimes describes herself as being sensitive. How can being "sensitive" cover up for anger and grudges?

    _____

    _____

10. How can a wife delight in evil?

    _____

    _____

11. Do you think being positive and dwelling on the good things is one aspect of rejoicing with the truth? Explain.

    _____

    _____

12. A wife is to be dependent and trusting. She is also to be responsible and prudent. Explain the balance.

_____

_____

13. Can you give an example of a Bible character who exhibited such balance? (1 Samuel 24)

_____

BALANCE

Wife is dependent and trusting　　　　　　**Wife is responsible and prudent**

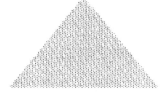

BALANCE

Chapter Thirteen
UNIQUELY YOU

"Lisa, how do you manage ... I mean how do you keep your self-esteem intact when Craig puts you down? I fall apart when my husband says anything negative. I feel so worthless. My self-esteem must be zero. What do you do to build yourself up?"

Lisa thought carefully. "Someone else asked me the same question. I guess my answer is that I concentrate on God instead of myself. I don't worry about my self-esteem. In my quiet time, I try to see myself as God sees me. He encourages me and corrects me. When you concentrate on knowing the truth about yourself and change to please God, you determine real self-worth."

The wonderful news is that any woman can focus on God. You don't have to be beautiful, intelligent, or talented. You can live in a grimy little house with six kids or in a palatial home on top of the hill. You can be sick, unhappy, or feeling badly about yourself, or be a successful career woman. When you focus on God, enjoy Him, and learn more about Him, you'll rejoice because ... the more you know God, the happier you will be. That is why you were created. You were created to glorify (mirror, obey, and please) God and enjoy Him forever.

- To put it another way, you are created to:

155

- Love God

- Reflect God in all actions and situations

- Give God credit at all times for His attributes

- Spread His fame

- Share the amazing news that God redeemed you in spite of your sins and unworthiness

- Enjoy Him and His creation

You were not created to:

- Spread your own good name

- Become someone in your own right

- Add something to God

- Feel good about yourself

Ironically, when you focus on God, you feel better about yourself. You learn you were created for a purpose. Loving and knowing God more each day doesn't mean you have to be "other worldly." In fact, you'll have eyes to see what you're supposed to be doing. Our God is very practical. When Christ was dying on the cross, He was thinking of His mother. He told her where to live. You too will learn what you should do. And God will surprise you.

WHERE DO YOU BEGIN WHEN YOU ARE BOWED DOWN WITH

NEGATIVES AND YOU FEEL DISCOURAGED AND
WORTHLESS? YOU TEAR DOWN BEFORE YOU BUILD UP. You
need an accurate view of yourself before you change and build up. You need
God's view of yourself. That's why you go to Him in your quiet time.

THE MESSED UP VIEW OF THE FOUNDATION OF YOUR
CHARACTER

1. First you throw out all the inaccuracies that are placed upon you.

If your husband snidely insinuates that you're "too religious," you toss
that out. If he calls you lazy or another family member calls you stupid, toss
that out. Ask God to help you see the truth. Perhaps you have been called

Rosemarie D. Malroy

certain things all your life and believe it, but it isn't true. Toss all the untruths out.

2. Then you recognize chinks in your foundation. These are weaknesses or sins—straw bricks. Toss them out by repentance and change.

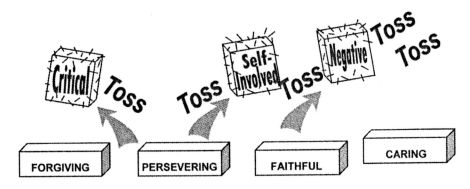

God is very gentle. He doesn't reveal all your straw bricks at once. He brings them out one at a time. Sometimes he uses your mate to help you zero in on one of your sins. That gives you a chance to replace that old straw brick with gold. It's hard, though. That's when you get depressed and discouraged. But if you have the picture clear—building your character so you can better reveal God—it won't hurt quite so much—a little less anyway.

3. NOW YOU BUILD UP!!! You proceed to replace your straw bricks with golden bricks of character and recognize your good points. Not so you can pat yourself on the back, but so you will honor God and become confident of a strong foundation to build your life on.

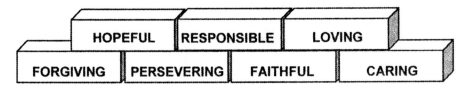

HOPEFUL	RESPONSIBLE	LOVING	
FORGIVING	PERSEVERING	FAITHFUL	CARING

Then you can house works for God utilizing your talents and accomplishing great things. Each house will be different.

Now that you've got your house in order, you can begin. You have learned the truth about yourself. You aren't as bad as some people say (you may be worse than others think) and you know your weaknesses.

Are you utilizing your talents? Have you recognized them and given God credit for them?

Mary, an older woman, felt depressed. Friends and family were starting new careers or working in the church. The care of her mother-in-law, limited finances, and a demanding husband kept her homebound.

"I'm not doing anything creative or making any money," she told her friend.

"What do you mean?" asked her friend. "You keep a nice house, make delicious meals, and are patient and loving to your mother-in-law. I think you deserve a crown."

Mary was encouraged to examine ways to feature her talents and take time to enjoy herself. She found that she enjoyed making bread in her bread maker and developed new recipes. She then contributed her bread to church functions and gave it as gifts to neighbors and friends.

She and her mother-in-law planted a special flower garden where they could sit and sip coffee and enjoy God's world. Mary also took more time for herself and attended different classes that she enjoyed.

In our society, unless you have a career, are paid for your work, or do big and dramatic projects, your work is considered meaningless. God doesn't see things that way. <u>The important thing is that you are where He wants you to be, so you can do what He wants you to do</u>. Sometimes the most inconsequential act at the right place and right time determines your use to God.

The widow at Zarephath was doing what she should have been doing. Famine had come to the land, and she had nothing left. She checked carefully through the house. No money or food could be found except enough flour and oil to make two patties of pita bread—one for herself and one for her son. Faithful to the end and still trusting God, she walked out of town to find some sticks for a fire to make their last meal. Can you imagine how helpless she must have felt? No food and no money, but she worked gathering little sticks. A voice called to her. Startled, she looked up to see the dramatic figure of the prophet Elijah standing there.

"Would you bring me a little water in a jar so I may have a drink?" he asked. As she was going to get it, he called, "And bring me, please, a piece of bread."

"As surely as the Lord your God lives," she replied, "I don't have any bread—only a handful of flour in a jar and a little oil in a jug. I am gathering a few sticks to take home and make a meal for myself and my son, that we may eat it—and die." (1 Kings 17:10b-12)

Elijah then told her to make him a cake of bread first and said that her flour and oil would not run out until the famine was over. So she fed Elijah. The widow at Zerphath was where she should have been. God used her to cook for the great prophet all during the famine. His life, the widow's, and her son's life were spared. In fact, later when her son died, God used the event to record His power for all times. He used Elijah to bring the son back to life. Imagine, a few extra steps to gather sticks placed her as an important woman in history.

Are you where you are supposed to be so you can utilize your talents and do what God wants you to do—whether it is cooking for prophets or designing buildings? Or do you feel slighted and hedged in by responsibilities with no understanding from your mate? Does God's thumb seem to be keeping you in place?

Rosemarie D. Malroy

C. S. Lewis addressed this problem in his book <u>The Great Divorce</u>. He said,

> I believe, to be sure, that any man (or woman) who reaches Heaven will find that what he abandoned (even in plucking out his right eye) was precisely nothing. That the kernel of what he was really seeking even in his most depraved wishes will be there, beyond expectation, waiting for him in "the High countries." (p. 6)

Lewis was saying that you may have to wait to do what you want. However, you can be sure that if you don't do it here, the good part of your desire will be found in heaven.

So, instead of being frustrated, find where God wants you to be and concentrate on your talents in that capacity utilizing them all.

RESPONSIBILITIES   TALENTS TO UTILIZE

To God   _____

To Husband   _____

To Children   _____

To Home   _____

To Job or Career   _____

To Society and Others   _____

EXAMPLE

RESPONSIBILITIES	TALENTS TO UTILIZE
To God	Go to church, teach Sunday school, quiet time, Bible study
To Husband	Cook healthful meals
To Children	Home school
To Home	Make curtains
To Job or Career	Write
To Society and Others	Vote, help at polls

Be sure to leave time for yourself. If you don't, you won't be able to perform your responsibilities joyfully and with a grateful heart. There is a balance.

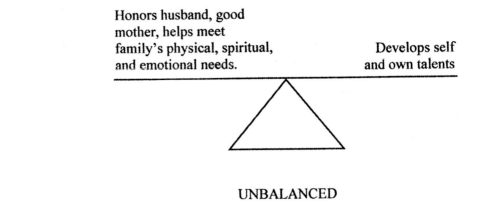

BALANCED

Honors husband, good
mother, helps meet
family's physical, spiritual,
and emotional needs.

Develops self
and own talents

UNBALANCED

FAMILY DOMINATED
Centers whole life around family
to the extent that she doesn't have
own identity. Such a servant that
she spoils her family not teaching
them to serve others.

SELFISH
not meeting
family's needs

Now that you've written out all your responsibilities and put your
talents to work, maybe you'll find that you need to cut back. You need time
for your health, recreation, grooming, and education.

BLOOM AND BECOME THE BEST THAT YOU CAN BE

1. Know the truth about yourself

2. Utilize your talents

3. Take time for yourself

4. Health

5. Grooming

6. Education

7. Recreation

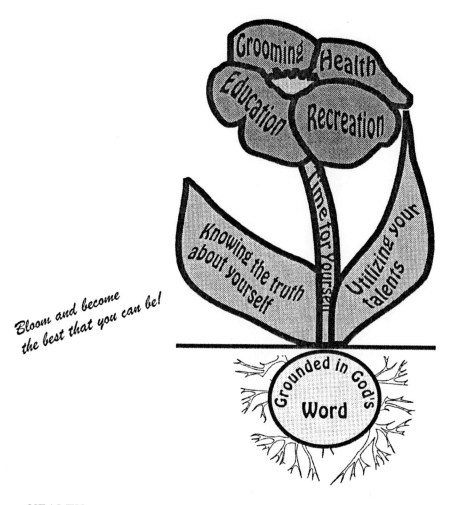

HEALTH

Your health is an important issue. Take time to exercise, eat properly,

and get enough rest and relaxation. Take care of your eyes and teeth and be sure you have a yearly check-up. If you have poor health, cut back wherever you can so you can complete your basic responsibilities and not overwork.

GROOMING

There are two important people to please concerning grooming—you and your husband. Don't cut back so much that you don't have at least one sharp outfit to wear. But don't overdo it either. 1 Peter 3:3&4 says that your beauty should not come from outward adornment, such as braided hair and the wearing of gold jewelry and fine clothes. Instead, it should be that of your inner self, the unfading beauty of a gentle and quiet spirit, which is of great worth in God's sight.

This Scripture means that you shouldn't depend on your physical beauty to win your husband. Good grooming is desirable, though. Perhaps a friend will sew you a dress or give you a permanent if you will take care of her children for a specific time. Shop wisely and hit sales. A woman feels better about herself when she is well-groomed. Figure out a good hair style for you and learn your best colors. It is important that you look nice for your husband. A neat, attractive woman makes life more enjoyable for any man.

EDUCATION

A Christian woman's continuing education continues until she dies. Your church provides classes for free. Take your classes seriously as if you were attending college and get the most out of them. If you apply the

Scriptures and study them, you will become a gentile, educated woman. Also, take other classes whenever they will improve your talents or help in your work. Most husbands respect a woman who improves her education. If your husband doesn't, don't let that keep you from improving yourself.

RECREATION

Remember to keep time to enjoy yourself. It is good for your attitudes. In our society, we can become so busy that life becomes a grueling treadmill. Widowed wives can get discouraged and depressed. A special hobby or sport can help you keep a proper perspective and keep you grateful for God's gifts. Maybe you and your husband can share a sport or hobby. This will help you to grow closer. It is important to do fun things together.

Reward yourself for jobs well done. After doing a difficult task, take ten minutes to do a crossword puzzle or read a chapter in a good book. Spice up life with little pleasures. Perhaps it is enjoying a cup of herbal tea while watching the sunrise. These special minutes of fun and rewards make the most difficult life more pleasant.

MINUTES OF REWARDS
Lisa's List

2-10 minutes	5-30 minutes	30 minutes to 1/2 day	1/2 day or more
Read catalogue	Read magazine	Paint picture	Go to gem show
Cup of tea	Read cookbook	Read book	Hike
Daydream	Watch TV	Relax with husband	Shop antiques
Read hobby magazine	Plan art piece	Hear tape/CD	Go to play
Plan fun for family	Write happy letter	Breakfast or lunch out	Visit model home
Kaleidoscope	Walk	Yard work	Concert
Puzzle	Dance to music	Go to library	Shop
Plan Christmas	Embroider	Go to mall	Art museum
Write wish list	Set goals	Make cards	Ballet
Plan Christmas gifts	Make flower arrangement	Change decorations	Beach
Look at art book	Check on mini-vacation	Bake cookies	Drive
Plan menu	Plan wardrobe	Bubblebath	Swim
Call friend	Read mail	Yard sale	Visit friends
Snack	Solitaire	Bookstore	Farmer's market
Nails	Plan garden	Picnic	Make gifts
		Games	Pick berries
			Party

Now make your own list.

	MINUTES OF REWARDS		
	_____ List		
2-10 minutes	5-30 minutes	30 minutes to 1/2 day	1/2 day or more

Each Christian woman is a flower slowly unfolding. You have special talents and traits that will blossom and perfume the earth. God has an appointed place for you. Be there to do your job and bloom.

CHAPTER THIRTEEN
BIBLE STUDY AND DISCUSSION

Read each verse and discuss how God's attributes or characteristics affect you. Do you have other favorite verses?

A GODLY WOMAN CENTERS ON GOD—NOT HERSELF

She concentrates on:

GOD INCARNATE—JESUS CHRIST
Your attitude should be the same as that of Christ Jesus:

6 Who being in very nature God, did not consider equality with God something to be grasped, 7 but made himself nothing, taking the very nature of a servant, being made in human likeness. 8 And being found in appearance as a man, he humbled himself and became obedient to death—even death on a cross! (Philippians 2:5-8)

THE MAJESTY OF GOD
The Lord reigns, he is robed in majesty; the Lord is robed in majesty and is armed with strength. The world is firmly established; it cannot be moved. (Psalm 93:1)

HIS WISDOM
Counsel and sound judgment are mine; I have understanding and power. (Proverbs 8:14) You guide me with your counsel. (Psalm 73:24a)

HIS LOVE AND GRACE
For he chose us in him before the creation of the world to be holy and blameless in his sight. In love 5 he predestined us to be adopted as his sons through Jesus Christ, in accordance with his pleasure and will—6 to the praise of his glorious grace, which he has freely given us in the One he loves. (Ephesians 1:4-6)

HIS JUSTICE
When the Son of Man comes in his glory, and all the angels with him, he will sit on his throne in heavenly glory. 32 All the nations will be gathered before him, and he will separate the people one from another as a shepherd separates the sheep from the goats. 33 He will put the sheep on his right and the goats on his left. (Matthew 25:31-33)

HIS SOVEREIGNTY
He was given authority, glory and sovereign power; all peoples, nations and men of every language worshiped him. His dominion is an everlasting dominion that will not pass away, and his kingdom is one that will never be destroyed. (Daniel 7:14)

CHAPTER THIRTEEN QUESTIONS

1. Review your responsibilities. Are you developing talents that will help you perform your responsibilities better?

    _____

2. Tell how you are working on one of your negative traits.

    _____

    _____

3. What are some of your positive traits?

    _____

    _____

4. Have you discovered false accusations about your character that you have believed?

    _____

Chapter Fourteen
ASSUMING SPIRITUAL RESPONSIBILITIES

Nothing can be more disastrous to a home than having no spiritual leadership. Even in Christian families, we see a decline in attention to God's ways. In our hectic lifestyle where many parents both work, spiritual matters get shoved aside out of sheer exhaustion.

Yet, we are in a warfare where spiritual forces of evil battle for our minds and souls. Our children are in jeopardy daily. Each family needs strong spiritual leadership. In God's order the husband is to be the spiritual leader. From Genesis to Revelation, He gives us examples—Abraham, Jacob, Joshua, Joseph, and Cornelius.

But what do you do when your husband has no spiritual interest and refuses to be the spiritual leader? God graciously gives the example of Eunice, Timothy's mother.

Eunice, a Jewish woman, married a Greek. Her mother, Lois, became the first Christian in the family. She shared her faith with her daughter who, in turn, became a Christian. Apparently, Eunice's husband wasn't interested in this "new religion," so he did not participate. But Eunice and her mother taught little Timothy from the time he was born. They shared their faith with him. Paul reminded Timothy of this in 2 Timothy 3:14-15:

173

But as for you [Timothy], continue in what you have learned and have become convinced of, because you know those from who you learned it, <u>and how from infancy you have known the holy Scriptures,</u> which are able to make you wise for salvation through faith in Christ Jesus. (emphasis added)

What a commendation for Eunice and Lois. Furthermore, Paul said their vibrant faith and the teaching they imparted to Timothy would keep him strong during his persecution. And it did. Timothy is known for all time as the faithful young pastor and co-worker of Paul.

How do you begin to produce your Timothys and Eunices? These special little ones you hold in your heart and arms are treasures for God. Will they be able to stand as Christians during persecution as did Timothy? By God's grace they will if you follow Eunice's example as spiritual leader.

DYING TO SELF

As a Christian woman, you fill in spiritually in the home. You are responsible for the spiritual care and growth of the family. What does that entail? The Christian husband and leader patterns himself after Christ's treatment of the church. Though he uses authority and issues rules in reasoning with his family, he is not dictatorial. He corrects them in a tender and loving way. <u>He dies to self.</u> (see Ephesians 5:25)

You assume that responsibility and go to God as your spiritual leader. You serve with love and show by example what it means to die to self. You give up your rights. The spiritual welfare of the family comes before your own personal wishes and desires.

Sara read Ephesians 5 slowly to herself.

"The husband here is so different from my husband. When I study to see how a husband is to be a spiritual leader, I am amazed. He is supposed to love his wife so much he will die for her. His love is a major part of his leadership. You know," she said sadly, "I don't think my husband would die for me. Last month when I was very sick with the flu, he was angry when I asked him to please go to the store and get me some aspirin."

There are many Saras in the world who feel unloved. Yet if you are one, and need to assume the burden of taking on your husband's spiritual responsibilities, Christ is with you. Remember, Christ becomes your loving spiritual husband. He is the spiritual leader of your home. His love and understanding fill the gap. That is why your quiet time is so important. You need to take time to realize Christ's presence and loving concern. He will lead you, and will guide you by His Word.

FINDING A CHURCH HOME

Christ also knows you need spiritual encouragement from others. That is why he instituted His church. The Bible says the place for Christians is the church. "And the Lord added to the church daily such as were being saved." (Acts 2:47b)

A church home provides wonderful support. Being the only Christian parent in the home is an added responsibility and an unnatural burden. Seeing the examples of Christian families will help. Members can also be spiritual fathers and mothers to your children as Paul "adopted" Timothy. Christ pours His love out to you through His church.

You probably already have a church home, but if you don't, here are some guidelines:

1. Find a church that believes the Bible is the infallible Word of God. You need Christians who can answer your questions from the Bible and help you apply it.

2. The members trust Jesus as Saviour.

3. Their lives show it—they imitate Christ.

4. It is not a worldly church. It isn't a church subjected to laws of human origin.

5. The church practices church discipline. It corrects those who commit flagrant sins.

Sixteen-year-old Joss acted confused. His mother was a devoted Christian, but his father thought spiritual matters were a waste of time. Torn between going on fun camping trips with his dad or the serious business of worship Sunday morning, he rebelled.

"I will do my own thing," he declared. The youth leader understood the boy's divided allegiance and zeroed in to be a spiritual father, easing Joss over the threshold to faith.

FINDING A SUPPORT GROUP

Sometimes in your church, you will find friends who understand your dilemma as a spiritually widowed wife. They will be your support group. Other times, family members or co-workers will fill in. Be sure they are Christians who will keep you balanced on God's Word. If you don't have anyone, pray for one friend. God will answer.

CHURCH ATTENDANCE

Taking your family to church without the support of your husband can be utterly exhausting. Yet it is essential for you and your family.

One pastor told how as a boy he hated the "dull" sermons. Yet when he got older, the "Hound of Heaven" drew him to Himself. Then the dull sermons fit into place. He had a solid foundation on which to prepare for the ministry.

It is amazing how much children absorb in a church service. They may not seem to be listening, but little minds are taking in many things. Also, a good Sunday school teacher can influence them for life as did the teacher of Dwight L. Moody.

PRACTICAL HINTS

1. Make Sunday morning attendance a habit, so no one will ask, "Are we going to church today?" Make it a given—we go to church each Sunday. Of course, there will be exceptions.

2. Help children take notes during the sermon. Draw pictures to help them understand.

3. Prepare the night before. Take baths then and have clean clothes ready.

4. Try to enlist your husband's cooperation even though he doesn't attend church.

5. Don't overdo church. Biblically, you are required to attend only one worship service on Sunday. Maybe you will serve the Lord better ministering to the man God gave you for a husband other parts of the day.

6. Make homecoming a pleasant time. Have little snacks ready if the family has to wait for dinner. Better yet, have dinner in the

oven or in a crock pot. Please your husband with the kind of meal he likes.

To best elicit the cooperation of your husband, don't make him seem like the "bad" guy. Do this by minimizing the "two camps" in your household. Show loving concern for his lack of interest, but don't emphasize that you are right and he is wrong. Instead put your emphasis on God's Word and exhibit your sincere faith. As the years go by and your children observe and get to know Christian men in the church, they will see how Christian families operate. They also will see how you apply your faith in hope of God's salvation.

For Mike and Lana, every Sunday morning had become a shouting match. Emotions ran high. Mike resented the fact that Lana went against his wishes and took the children to church instead of spending time with him. Lana resented him for not taking the spiritual leadership.

"Where's my coffee beans?" Mike shouted.

"I don't know," Lana exclaimed in exasperation. "I've got two kids and myself to get ready."

"Can't you forget this church stuff one Sunday and relax?" Mike yelled at her.

"You're worthless when it comes to training our children," Lana cried.

CREATING A LOVING CHRISTIAN HOME

Lana had a lot of work to do to create a stable environment where her little ones would grow in Christ. Seeing their parents fight over church was not good.

Paul spoke highly of Eunice and Lois, so we know they created a loving Christian home. In following Eunice's example, you can't lash out because of the added Christian responsibilities you bear.

God corrected Lana through His Word and she knew she had to change. First she tried to understand Mike's point of view. Mike considered Sunday his day to relax. In his childhood home, everyone slept in on Sunday. Then they had a leisurely breakfast of ham and eggs. Lana figured out how she could compromise. She planned a brunch after church, and then everyone relaxed the rest of the day.

She also made Mike the most important person in her life by:

> Taking time to do what he wanted to do
>
> Not making phone calls to her friends in his presence
>
> Viewing her church activities as her recreation
>
> Trying not to retaliate when he put her down
>
> Not comparing him to other Christian men
>
> Not becoming infatuated with men she admired

One other important thing she did was to get enough rest so she could be a good sex partner.

Lana died to self. She cut out desired activities in order to be available for her husband. Because she did so, Mike respected her wishes to attend church on Sunday mornings.

Creating a loving Christian home can be expensive, yet it is necessary for the spiritual growth of your family. Cynthia found it cost her a new home. Two days a week working was all she could afford to do and still be able to maintain the spiritual and physical needs of her husband and children. However, it paid off. This day finds all her family loyal Christians.

PRACTICAL MATTERS FOR SPIRITUAL GROWTH
TABLE GRACE

Teaching your children to thank God for His good blessings is important. Thanking God for the food before them is a means to do so. However, don't use this time to "chastise" Dad by saying such things as, "Help Dad go to church." He will deeply resent it. If he becomes angry about taking time before the meal, say a short thanks after. Weigh the benefits of saying grace. If it becomes a bone of contention, it may be best to wait for further guidance.

FAMILY DEVOTIONS

Family devotions can indelibly mark your child. They even help your husband if he listens. In fact, they are essential to Christian training. Some husbands resent being present during devotions, so it is up to you to find a time slot where you can privately teach your children. Read a Bible story before bedtime. Leave time for questions. Some of the best discussions come about because kids are trying to prevent "lights out." Reviewing the child's day enables you to pray with him about his concerns.

It is very beneficial to read a chapter in a "fun story" too. This includes great Christian literature. "Pilgrim's Progress" and many other books can be read and discussed. Get a book list from your church librarian.

TITHING

God blesses those who tithe. It is a practical expression of their genuine love. However, many widowed wives don't have that option. Perhaps you can tithe the household money or the money you earn. Some women tithe their time in service to God.

HOUSE GUESTS

Maybe your home can be open to traveling ministers, missionaries, or other Christians. This can be a wonderful contact for your husband. His getting to know Christian men and their way of thinking can be a means of God's blessing. Quietly let your guests know beforehand your husband's lack of spiritual interest. Don't get excited and expect some miracle. Relax and have fun together. This experience is also wonderful for your children.

Being the only Christian parent is a great responsibility. Dying to self, standing firm on the Word of God, and creating a loving Christian home where you express your faith is no easy matter. Yet as Eunice was blessed with her Timothy, so you, too, will find God's blessings. It will be in His own time and in His own way. The joys will billow down through the ages and into worlds unknown.

CHAPTER FOURTEEN
BIBLE STUDY AND DISCUSSION

Discuss each verse and tell how it can help you assume the spiritual responsibilities in your home.

I have been reminded of your sincere faith, which first lived in your grandmother Lois and in your mother Eunice and, I am persuaded, now lives in you also. (2 Timothy 1:5)

Finally, be strong in the Lord and in his mighty power. 11 Put on the full armor of God so that you can take your stand against the devil's schemes. 12 For our struggle is not against flesh and blood, but against the rulers, against the authorities, against the powers of this dark world and against the spiritual forces of evil in the heavenly realms. 13 Therefore put on the full armor of God, so that when the day of evil comes, you may be able to stand your ground, and after you have done everything, to stand. 14 Stand firm then, with the belt of truth buckled around your waist, with the breastplate of righteousness in place, and your feet fitted with the readiness that comes from the gospel of peace. 16 In addition to all this, take up the shield of faith, with which you can extinguish all the flaming arrows of the evil one. 17 Take the helmet of salvation and the sword of the Spirit, which is the word of God. 18 And pray in the Spirit on all occasions with all kinds of prayers and requests. With this in mind, be alert and always keep on praying for all saints. (Ephesians 6:10-18)

We will not hide them from their children; we will tell the next generation the praiseworthy deeds of the Lord, his power, and the wonders he has done. (Psalm 78:4)

CHAPTER FOURTEEN QUESTIONS

1. Tell how persistence and consistence might help you stabilize your family.

    _____

    _____

    _____

    How did it help Lois and Eunice?

    _____

    _____

2. Tell why love and humility are so important in leadership.

    _____

    _____

    _____

3. Do you think you may have to take a stand against the devil's schemes when you assume your spiritual responsibility? Explain.

    _____

    _____

    _____

Rosemarie D. Malroy

4. How do you remain strong in the Lord?

_____

_____

5. What does each piece of armor represent?

Belt _____

Breastplate _____

Feet _____

Shield _____

Helmet _____

Sword _____

WAYS I CAN ASSUME SPIRITUAL RESPONSIBILITIES IN OUR

HOME

1. _____

2. _____

3. _____

4. _____

5. _____

6. _____

Chapter Fifteen
ASSUMING THE SUPPORTIVE ROLE

Exhausted, Lisa surveyed the living room. Her eyes rested on the pile of books she had asked Todd, her teenage son, to take to school for the book sale several days before.

"Todd, take those books down to the school this minute," she commanded.

"I can't," he said. "Dad told me to get his fishing gear ready."

"I don't care what your father said. Get those books to the school!"

Lisa's stomach knotted up. She felt angry and bitterness seeped into her soul. *Why was she the one who had to ramrod order around here? Craig knew this was the weekend of the school festival.* A cold hardness settled in her being. *She'd forget about help from Craig. Fishing! She'd see to things herself.*

When men avoid their responsibilities, women take over. Often times the woman assumes leadership in all matters even though the man performs part of his duties as father and head of the house. When the woman assumes more responsibility than is actually required of her, the man then backs off, leaving her the full load.

A woman is not to usurp either a husband's headship or his responsibilities. She is to be a helper. (Genesis 2:18) She is to fill in for him where he needs it.

SOCIETY'S ORDER
OF HEADSHIP IN FAMILIES

WIFE
Head

CHILDREN
Left mostly to themselves

HUSBAND

GOD'S ORDER FOR THE FAMILY

CHRIST
"Head" of the husband
Lord of the family

HUSBAND
"Head" of the wife
Chief authority over the children

WIFE
Helpmeet to the husband (Genesis 2:18)
Secondary authority over the children

CHILDREN
Obedient to parents

CAN'T DO IT ALL

Many women in today's society have been misled, deceived, and hoodwinked. They are told they can do everything. Basically, they think they don't need a husband. They think they can be provider, mother, father, spiritual leader, and head of the household.

What has happened to bring this about? Men have bowed out. More and more, they are not assuming their responsibilities as head of the family or as provider or spiritual leader. Millions of women struggle as single parents trying to do it all and finding it usually doesn't work. Either they give up—not fulfilling the responsibilities it takes to create a stable family—or they run amuck trying to provide.

Stop, spiritually widowed wife! Learn from God's Word. Let your husband assume any part of headship he will. Encourage him. Respect him. Compliment him. Submit to him. Even if he doesn't do things the way you think they should be done, give him credit for trying.

When you are in a situation where a man sometimes fulfills his responsibilities and sometimes not, it can be very discouraging. It may seem easier to take over and do it yourself.

Lisa struggled with the boxes for the school festival.

"What are you doing?" Craig asked.

"I'm getting ready for the school festival. You seem to be going fishing. Somebody had to do the work around here," she said bitterly.

"Come on," said Craig. "We're going fishing after we set up everything for the festival. Are you going to let me help you?"

Anger swirled inside Lisa. She felt like saying "no." However, she mumbled something and sunk into a chair.

Craig looked at her. "You look beat," he said laughing. "You are so stubborn. You always jump to conclusions."

"Dad," Todd said, "I didn't get the fishing gear ready. Mom made me take the books to school."

Lisa blushed, remembering her words. "I'm sorry. He didn't take in the books last week like I told him to do," she said.

Lisa had inadvertently usurped Craig's head as father and taken over his responsibility in the community.

It takes faith to trust a man when part of the time he neglects his responsibilities. However, sometimes it is better to let things go undone in hope he'll come through rather than assume he won't. It sends a message to him that you expect him to do his duty.

In his book <u>The Christian Family</u>, Larry Christenson says,

> It is the husband, not the wife, who is primarily responsible for what goes on in the home, the community, and the church. When he deserts this role, or when the wife

usurps it, both the home and the community outside the home suffer for it. (p. 37)

Today our homes and communities are suffering. You as a widowed wife, instead of trying to take over, can give your husband every opportunity to fulfill his duties. Sometimes you have to take over, but keep in mind that your goal is to let him do his responsibilities so you can do yours.

WIFE'S RESPONSIBILITY

What is a wife's responsibility? Primarily, it is to give of herself to her husband, family, and home. She is to support her husband and fit into his plans. Her home and family are her central concern. That doesn't mean she can't have other responsibilities, but they are secondary. The woman in Proverbs 31 is a good example. A busy woman, she helped the poor, dealt in real estate, ran a small business selling goods she produced, managed servants and employees, sewed, and made her home beautiful. She shopped and cooked and took good care of the home. She also was godly and wise. She instructed her family well. She allowed her husband time to pursue his career and excel in his work. She supported him in his activities in the community and church. She also let her husband receive the recognition of leader.

This does not describe a woman who spends a great deal of time in self-centered activities. This woman fears God. In other words, she submits to

God by honoring her husband. Because of her diligence and good training, her family calls her blessed and praises her.

Have you known a woman like this? Look around. She is still here. Maybe she doesn't make a big splash with a fancy career or name recognition. However, in the end—and for generations to come—she will be praised. See if you can find women such as this in different stages of their lives.

Now, how can you adapt some of this wise woman's actions to your life? Notice she works with "eager hands." Can you do so in your home? Today, many young women work a nine-to-five job outside the home. They think it is the thing to do. They get a little money, but by the time they pay the sitter, pay for transportation, buy new clothes for work, and buy ready-made food, they have very little left over. Their home, husband, and children suffer.

Is there any other way you can make the same amount of take-home money and be able to make your home the center? It takes a lot of work with "eager hands" to cook from scratch, have a garden (she "plants a vineyard"), decorate the house ("makes coverings for her bed"), sew clothes, and produce a small income from your home base. In our society you won't get recognition for it. With a sneer, people may say, "She's just a homemaker!" But will God be pleased that your home is the center? Will your husband be happier? Will you be better able to adapt to him? Will you have more time to train your children?

If you desire to work at home, be creative. Seek out some need and fill it. Can you teach a class? Do interior decorating? Sell a service? Do secretarial work? Make crafts to sell? Take care of another child?

If you have a rewarding career, maybe you can cut back and work part-time while your children are small. Then you will have more time to:

- Make a delightful home

- Train your children

- Fulfill a supportive role to your husband

- Be romantic

- Be a good Christian witness to friends and family

- Help your church and community

Perhaps your husband demands you work full time. So be it. Make the best of it or pray to God to intervene. It is wonderful how God gives you the desires of your heart. If you can prove you can make as much money working at home, your husband may reconsider. Maybe you feel it is very important to keep up your career that you have sacrificed to obtain. If you have children, unless you have support and help from your husband, it is very difficult to keep up your responsibilities. Remember, you have more responsibilities than your sisters in Christ whose husbands help in the spiritual training. You need to be willing to give up your career if you are unable to perform all your duties.

Many marriages have dissolved because a woman has neglected her husband because of her career. Children have gone astray because of little training and no example of putting God first. A career that causes the demise of a marriage or the neglect of children does not please God. Even in the secular world, young professional women are putting their careers on hold when they have preschoolers. They know that only they can instill in their children their value system and give them the nurturing and bonding they need.

Whatever a woman does, if her goal and wish is to be supportive to her husband and obey God, God will see her heart and be pleased. A husband usually responds positively when he knows his wife supports his headship. What if he doesn't? Then do your best and don't feel guilty. Trust the Lord.

Is the Bible really God's letter to us? When society ridicules the principle of God's order for the family, does that mean it doesn't apply today? Strong families down through the centuries have submitted to God's rule. From Genesis to Revelation, from Christ's ascension to the present, families have obeyed God in such matters. Today, many families do not. Do they look like strong, happy families? Are their homes pleasant places to be? Do children respect and obey parents, and do parents love and discipline children? Do wives respect husbands and do husbands love wives? God desires this for families.

<h2 style="text-align:center">SUBMIT TO YOUR HUSBAND</h2>

Even though your husband doesn't recognize Christ as his Head, you are commanded to submit to him. There is a reason for it. God uses your husband to protect you, balance you, and help you.

Wives, submit to your husbands, as is fitting in the Lord. (Colossians 3:18)

<h2 style="text-align:center">NOT A DOORMAT</h2>

Does that mean you should be a doormat? Indeed not! Neither do you do anything that will dishonor God. You are equal with your husband. (Galatians 3:27-28) In the order of authority you submit, but God expects you to use your mind and energy. You yield humble and intelligent obedience to an ordained power of authority, but you use your judgment, wisdom, and opinion to save your husband from foolish mistakes. You don't murmur a "yes, dear" in servility, but reason with him in all matters, making your case as strongly as you can. You meet him with help.

Billy Graham's wife, Ruth Bell Graham, in her book It's My Turn, says this

> I have met wives who did not dare to disagree with their husbands. I have met wives who were not permitted to disagree with their husbands. In each case, the husband suffered. Either he became insufferably conceited, made

195

unwise judgments, tended to run roughshod over other people, or was just generally off-balance. However, it is a good thing to know how to disagree and when.

Here are a few suggestions out of my own experience: First, define the issue (and make sure it is worth disagreeing over); next, watch your tone of voice and be courteous (don't interrupt, and avoid rude, unkind, or unnecessarily personal remarks); third, stick to the subject; fourth, stick to facts; and fifth, concede graciously ...

Nor does it pay to argue with your husband unless you are looking your very best. (p. 54)

Ruth Graham is an example of a godly woman who supported her husband 100 percent. She had many happy years doing so. However, she had hard times too. Taking care of five children alone in an isolated house in the country, often for weeks at a time while he traveled the world evangelizing was not easy. When he did come home, he often brought guests to be entertained. Ruth felt he should spend more time alone with his family, but she submitted to his work, struggling with the responsibility of raising her family. She said, "This job of training five little Grahams to be good soldiers of Jesus Christ is too big for me, who is not a good soldier myself." But she persevered, depending on God.

One time Billy wanted her to take the children quite a distance to regularly attend the nearest Baptist church. At the time she was taking them to the nearby Presbyterian church where she was a member and where her parents attended. They helped her take the children to church and when one was sick, she could stay home.

She decided she would remain at the Presbyterian church. There is a time to say no. When you are delegated responsibility and then required to do something that you feel will hurt you in fulfilling that responsibility, it is up to you to let your husband know your limits.

Ruth is a strong woman whom God used greatly. She said, "Adapting to our husbands never implies the annihilation of our creativity, rather the blossoming of it." (p. 55)

It is interesting that in later years, the thing Billy Graham regretted most is that he didn't take more time to raise his family.

Widowed wives aren't the only ones who have their problems. But if you hang in there adapting to your husband's needs, God will honor you. Think how He honored Ruth and how He used her husband.

CHAPTER FIFTEEN

BIBLE STUDY AND DISCUSSION

Read and discuss. Is home her center?

The Wife of Noble Character

> A wife of noble character who can find?
> She is worth far more than rubies.
> Her husband has full confidence in her
> and lacks nothing of value.
> She brings him good, not harm,
> all the days of her life.
> She selects wool and flax
> and works with eager hands.
> She is like the merchant ships,
> bringing her food from afar.
> She gets up while it is still dark;
> she provides food for her family
> and portions for her servant girls.
> She considers a field and buys it;
> out of her earnings she plants a vineyard.
> She sets about her work vigorously;
> her arms are strong for her tasks.
> She sees that her trading is profitable,
> and her lamp does not go out at night.
> In her hand she holds the distaff
> and grasps the spindle with her fingers.
> She opens her arms to the poor
> and extends her hands to the needy.
> When it snows, she has no fear for her household;
> for all of them are clothed in scarlet.
> She makes coverings for her bed;
> she is clothed in fine linen and purple.
> Her husband is respected at the city gate,
> where he takes his seat among the elders of the land.
> She makes linen garments and sells them,
> and supplies the merchants with sashes.
> She is clothed with strength and dignity;
> she can laugh at the days to come.

She speaks with wisdom,
and faithful instruction is on her tongue.
She watches over the affairs of her household
and does not eat the bread of idleness.
Her children arise and call her blessed;
her husband also, and he praises her:
"Many women do noble things,
but you surpass them all."
Charm is deceptive, and beauty is fleeting;
but a woman who fears the Lord is to be praised.
Give her the reward she has earned,
and let her works bring her praise at the city gate.
(Proverbs 31:10-31)

CHAPTER FIFTEEN QUESTIONS

1. Proverbs 31:10-31 describes a wife of noble character. Why
    does her husband have full confidence in her?

    _____

    _____

2. How does she center her life around her husband, home, and
    family?

    _____

    _____

3. Our society disregards the importance of women in a supportive
    role to their husbands. Do you think the independence of
    woman has undermined the family? Why or why not?

    _____

4. Do you feel it is demeaning to be a homemaker in our society? If so, why?

_____

_____

5. Do you think a woman's fear of divorce is one reason she rejects the idea of being submissive to her husband? As a Christian woman married to a non-Christian, you are not insulated from desertion. How does your obedience in being a submissive wife show your fear of God?

_____

_____

_____

6. Jan refused to move when her husband was transferred because it would jeopardize her career. What godly principle is she breaking?

_____

7. What are the roles the woman in Proverbs performed?

_____

_____

_____

8. Do you think her home was a pleasant place to be?

    _____

    Do you think her family enjoyed being at home?
    _____ What makes you think so? _____

    _____

9. Do you think the Scriptures imply the reason her husband takes

    his place among the leaders is because his wife supported him in

    his work and endeavors? Why or why not?

    _____

    _____

Rosemarie D. Malroy

.

Chapter Sixteen
WITNESSING IN THE HOME

God's way for you to witness to your husband is the design of a Creator. He knows and understands the workings of men's minds and hearts. He says:

> Wives, in the same way be submissive to your husbands so that if any of them do not believe the word, they may be won over without talk by the behavior of their wives, when they see the purity and reverence of your lives. (1 Peter 3:1-2)

Darlene frowned. "It sounds easy to keep one's mouth shut and let God work," she said, "but it isn't easy for me. It irritates me to no end to come home from church and see my husband unshaven with a can of beer in his hand watching the football game. I come home all excited about knowing God more and wanting to spread the gospel, and there my husband sits. Sometimes I want to shake him and make him wake up. It's so hard to come home and not give him a 'good sermon.'"

For some women, not "preaching" is very difficult. Yet if you redirect your energies as God tells you, it will be easier. First, know that God is the one who saves—you don't. You need to cooperate with Him and do things His way. "No one can come to me unless the Father who sent me draws him, and I will raise him up at the last day." (John 6:44)

Are you discouraged when you look at your husband? He may not show any interest at all in the gospel. In fact, he may show a lot of antagonism towards it. Many men do not like help from anyone. Neither do they like being told they are sinners. "But the natural man receiveth not the things of the Spirit of God: for they are foolishness unto him: neither can he know them, because they are spiritually discerned." (1 Corinthians 2:14 KJV)

God gives you hope for the man in your life. He says, "I will give you a new heart and put a new spirit in you; I will remove from you your heart of stone and give you a heart of flesh. (Ezekiel 36:26)

WAIT ON GOD

The first constructive thing you can do is wait on God to give your husband a new heart. God is sovereign. He has everything under control. He works in His own way and time. You do not know for sure if God will save your mate, but to trust is better than to doubt.

TRUST GOD AND AVOID FEAR

Nothing will deliver you from your distress except a firm belief that all events are in the hands of God.

> Are not two sparrows sold for a penny? Yet not one of them will fall to the ground apart from the will of your Father. And even the very hairs of your head are all numbered. So don't be afraid: you are worth more than many sparrows. (Matthew 10:29-31)

You may not understand God's ways. But God has always worked in mysteries. No one in the Old Testament imagined how God would bring about man's salvation. They were expecting an earthly king—not Christ dying on the cross. So, too, you cannot know how God will work in your husband's life. It is a mystery. Don't trust in yourself or put much importance in your fears but realize that your all-powerful God is filled with mercy and will work as He sees fit.

You can expect difficulties, God's delays, and even God's silence. Psalm 88 teaches you to continue to pray even when you are despairing. It is Christ's way to teach you to be faithful.

HOW TO WITNESS BY BEING PURE, REVERENT, AND HAVING A GENTLE AND QUIET SPIRIT

Now you are ready to witness God's way. You haven't intimidated your husband with your talk about God or the Bible. You haven't clobbered your husband over the head with truth expecting him to appreciate it (at least for a while). Rather, you court him in love. You enjoy God so much and practice His truth in your life to such an extent that hopefully he, too, will be drawn to your marvelous Lord and Saviour. But how long does this have to go on without any results? Surely something will happen soon.

205

Lisa read 1 Peter 3 for the millionth time, it seemed. No tears came any more. When she was younger, she felt more inspired and not so tired. Now she felt loud and ugly—not gentle and quiet. Craig was better than he used to be but he still caused her pain. The night before he had been unreasonable and mean. The kids were angry at him too.

A brick wall seemed to channel her back to unhappy days in their lives, blocking out any happiness. <u>The bricks of bitterness, idealism, demand for happiness, and a critical spirit were preventing Lisa from having the right spirit.</u>

BITTERNESS

Lisa's stormy thoughts whirled as she read Psalm 88, her Scripture for the day. Verse 6 said, "You have put me in the lowest pit." That's exactly how Lisa felt but how did the psalmist dare tell God that?

Lisa wrote in her notebook: "I need to be honest. I am angry at my husband and bitter that he is not a Christian. Why, God? I've tried hard to witness your way. I feel you've put me in a pit."

With God's help, Lisa purged herself from bitterness. She told God exactly how she felt. Then she thought hopeful and beautiful thoughts. She also made a conscious effort to be thankful.

BALANCE

PURGE YOURSELF FROM BITTERNESS

Tell God exactly how you feel. (Lamentations 3:19-26)	**Think on good things so you can do good things. (Philippians 4:8)**

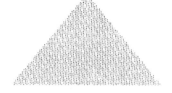

IDEALISM

To have wonderful goals and to want the very best is great. But when idealism encases you so that you can't accept your loved ones the way they are, it is detrimental. Nothing in this world is perfect. Idealism demands that it be so. It is unrealistic. Real love accepts the whole person but concentrates on the positive and encourages. Idealism tends to focus on the negative. It looks for imperfections, finds them, and then is unsatisfied.

DEMAND FOR HAPPINESS

When you demand happiness, it will flee from you. You make your own happiness. You do what you can do, then enjoy what you have.

A CRITICAL SPIRIT

It is easy to have a critical spirit, especially when things don't go your way. You want a good Christian husband and home. When he hinders that purpose, a common reaction is to zero in on his imperfections. Then a critical spirit prevails. Instead, concentrate on yourself. Aim at being pure, reverent, and gentle. Do this by backing off and looking at the whole picture. God is the one to change your husband's heart. You strengthen yourself to cooperate in the long term. Avoid the passions of the moment.

Lisa found one area of her life where she could overcome all four hindrances and be a good witness to her husband.

No bitterness—She turned his energetic, spontaneous ways into an asset instead of a negative, even though he didn't show her consideration. When he wanted the family to go with him, they went when they could.

No idealism—She adapted to his spur of the moment ideas. She left her work undone.

No critical spirit—She preferred to plan ahead but didn't complain.

No demand for happiness—She didn't expect to always have a great time. She was surprised to find out how many good times their family had together.

Are there any times when a wife should witness by speech to her husband? 1 Peter 3:15b-16a says, "Always be prepared to give an answer to everyone who asks you to give the reason for the hope that you have. But do this with gentleness and respect."

When you obey God's Word and do things His way, your husband is going to notice the difference between you and others. When your obedience elicits questions, be ready to answer him with gentleness and respect. Your goal for your silent witness is for this to happen. Don't be discouraged if it doesn't happen, however. God in His power and might works in many ways. Even though you don't see any results for your obedience, make pleasing God your end.

Rosemarie D. Malroy

CHAPTER SIXTEEN
BIBLE STUDY AND DISCUSSION

1 Peter 3:1-4 is explicit instructions for those who are married to men who do not believe the "word" or Bible. Study it again and discuss. Also, read and discuss the Scripture in Philippians.

> Wives, in the same way be submissive to your husbands so that, if any of them do not believe the word, they may be won over without talk by the behavior of their wives, 2 when they see the purity and reverence of your lives. 3 Your beauty should not come from outward adornment, such as braided hair and wearing of gold jewelry and fine clothes. 4 Instead, it should be that of your inner self, the unfading beauty of a gentle and quiet spirit, which is of great worth in God's sight. 5 For this is the way the holy women of the past who put their hope in God used to make themselves beautiful. They were submissive to their own husbands, 6 like Sarah, who obeyed Abraham and called him her master. You are her daughters if you do what is right and do not give way to fear. (1 Peter 3:1-4)

> Rejoice in the Lord always. I will say it again: Rejoice! 5 Let your gentleness be evident to all. The Lord is near. 6 Do not be anxious about anything, but in everything, by prayer and petition, with thanksgiving, present your requests to God. 7 And the peace of God, which transcends all understanding, will guard your hearts and your minds in Christ Jesus.
> 8 Finally, brothers, whatever is true, whatever is noble, whatever is right, whatever is pure, whatever is lovely, whatever is admirable—if anything is excellent or praiseworthy—think about such things. 9 Whatever you have learned or received or heard from me, or seen in me—put it into practice. And the God of peace will be with you. (Philippians 4:4-9)

210

CHAPTER SIXTEEN QUESTIONS

1. Describe how 1 Peter 3:1-4 goes against nearly everything expressed on TV.

   _____

   _____

   How does the emphasis on the physical instead of the spiritual in our society influence attitudes?

   _____

   _____

2. What four virtues should a woman exhibit when she is witnessing to her husband at home?

   a. _____

   b. _____

   c. _____

   d. _____

3. Why do you think God tells a Christian woman to witness to her husband by her behavior instead of her tongue?

   _____

   _____

   _____

4. Why does God want us to think on good things?

_____

_____

5. God commands us to rejoice. How can you do so when you have many problems and a husband who doesn't love God?

_____

6. Why shouldn't you worry?

_____

_____

7. When you make requests to God what else should you do?

_____

_____

8. What else will God give you if you ask Him for your needs and thank Him?

_____

_____

THINK ON THESE THINGS

What is:	Describe an Example You See in Your Life
1. True	1. _____
2. Noble	2. _____

3. Right

4. Pure

5. Lovely

6. Admirable

7. Excellent

8. Praiseworthy

3. _____

4. _____

5. _____

6. _____

7. _____

8. _____

Rosemarie D. Malroy

Chapter Seventeen
TRAINING IN THE HOME
by Juanita Rolph

Lisa usually found joy in listening to Christian music as she worked around her home. But today a piece had touched her heart in a way she couldn't shake off. A group had sung "David's Lamentation" with music by William Billings. She could hear David's broken heart in the group's voices as the song progressed. How he had grieved for his dead son. "O my son Absalom! My son, my son Absalom! If only I had died instead of you... O Absalom, my son, my son!" (2 Samuel 18:33b)

The more Lisa pondered on why so many of David's children had walked away from God's ways, the more she felt the need to look into his story a bit. After all, God warned in Psalm 89:30-32, "If his [David's] sons forsake my law and do not follow my statutes, if they violate my decrees and fail to keep my commands, I will punish their sin with the rod, their iniquity with flogging."

She didn't want to make the same mistakes in raising her children that David had made. Picking up her Bible, she turned to 2 Samuel and began to read with a whole new fascination.

Certainly David had loved his children. He went up to his chambers and wept over Absalom's death—even though Absalom had tried to usurp the kingdom from his dad, the king. Again, David had wept over Amnon's death, in spite of the fact he'd raped his own half sister, David's daughter.

Lisa used 2 Samuel for her devotions for nearly a month. Each day she entered into her journal those things which the Lord laid on her heart as important factors toward raising children who will choose to live by God's absolute standards.

DAVID MARRIED PAGAN WOMEN

Finally a picture began to form: <u>Many of David's wives were from surrounding pagan tribes</u>. They brought with them their own gods and types of religions. This meant their children were torn between the pagan gods of their mothers and the God Jehovah of their father, the king.

Lisa realized this wasn't so different from a contemporary Christian and non-Christian couple trying to parent. Today's non-Christian often worships sports, money, prestige, education, etc. She saw while the pagan gods were totally wrong, attitude can make false gods resulting in not following God also.

She was trying to raise her children in a godly home. What lesson was here for her? She noted in Genesis 24:3 that Abraham made his servant swear not to let Isaac have a wife from among the Canaanites, <u>among whom they dwelt</u>.

Uh huh. When children reach marriageable age, they will choose a mate from among their acquaintances. Since parents in our culture don't select the mates outright, it behooves the parents, then, to place the children in Christian environments where those they meet will hopefully have God's standards. This may mean the sacrifice and expense of a Christian school clear through to Christian college. It may mean sacrificing the convenience of a church home nearby to find a church which has an active, but still Bible-based, youth group. It means making your home open to your children's friends so you know their friends and know the developing attitudes. It means extra time spent supervising other children.

Lisa realized all of the above isn't enough, either. It has to be accompanied by persistent prayer from the time of infancy, that God, even then, is raising up exactly the right mate for one's child.

DAVID NEGLECTED TRAINING IN THE HOME

Also Lisa wondered, 'How often did David take a meal with each family?' He was off on his war campaigns a good share of each year. When he was home, his kingly duties called. Besides, each wife lived in her own apartment with her little matriarchal family unit. He could be with only one at a time. It meant his children were, essentially, single parented.

Now certainly many fine men and women have been raised by single parents. But it wasn't God's plan that it be done that way. Any parent who has had the task knows how much easier it is to share the responsibility of child-raising with a spouse.

But back to the family meal. It's around the table where leisurely conversation can be developed. Lisa knew this was not the time for discipline, but rather to explore ideas, to develop a family identity, to learn one's roots, to share the highlights of the day, to let God's absolutes soak in over the course of the years.

In many families, one meal a day is sacrosanct as far as every member of the family being present. Often, breakfast can most easily be arranged. Everyone learns to get up early enough to be at the table in time for a leisurely meal and family devotions before going out into the harsh world.

Lisa knew Craig wouldn't stand still for that. She determined to have devotions with the children at lunch. But she did resolve to discuss with Craig the importance of a family meal together. She gave the discussion a great deal of planning and prayer before letting it happen.

Craig determined he would try to be home so they could sit down for evening dinner as a family unit. It meant no television and no reading materials. Rather, there would be an effort to develop the fine art of good conversation.

Together they laid the rules:

1. The phone would be switched to the answering machine for one hour or until the family time was completed.

2. The only reading material allowed would be if someone were bringing something to quote for the sake of discussion.

3. No television, but quiet classical background music could be played.

4. Clients, business, committee meetings, church functions, etc. would be scheduled later in the evening or the next day.

5. Yes, sometimes friends and guests would be present at the meal.

6. No discipline would take place at the table other than the teaching of good table manners.

7. All conversation would be directed to all persons present.

8. No interruptions allowed when someone is speaking.

9. The long-term purpose would be to have a relaxed family time for exploring ideas and developing family roots and value systems.

It pleased Lisa that Craig was willing to make the effort to rearrange his evenings in order to put family first. She remembered to thank God for this and to give Him the glory for preparing Craig's heart for the conversation they had on the subject. Now she would have to trust God and continue to pray that Craig would keep his word and actually comply with the rules they'd established together.

As for devotions, she decided to use suggestions from The Parenting Bible published by Zondervan Publishing House (Grand Rapids, Michigan). It suggests devotions should:

1. Involve the children as participants

2. Focus on life issues important to the family

3. Be brief and not preachy

The Parenting Bible offers a one-year plan for family devotions and includes a weekly "HelpLine" and "FamilyFun" activity. They remind each family member that the Lord is present in the home.

Set the correct example for children. David's "lifestyle example" was harmful. He thought he had to have Bathsheba in his bed. It's only logical to assume that his children heard about how brother Solomon came to be. After all, it's human nature to talk.

So is it any wonder when Solomon came to power that his downfall was an excess of women—or polygamy, if you will?

DAVID WAS LAX IN DISCIPLINE

Discipline. It's recorded in 1 Kings 1:6 that David apparently was lax in disciplining his children. Adonijah's father (David) never interfered with him by asking, "Why do you behave as you do?"

Again, when Tamar was pleading with her brother not to rape her, she said, "Please speak to the king; he will not keep me from being married to you." (2 Samuel 13:13) The implication is that anything requested by the children was granted.

Children who are truly loved are disciplined in order to teach self-discipline, for only then can there be happiness in their lives. One dear grandmother always said, "If children step on your toes when they're little, they'll step on your heart when they're big." And the Scriptures certainly advocate discipline. Proverbs 19:18 says, "Discipline your son, for in that there is hope; do not be a willing party to his death."

Lisa pondered over how not disciplining leads to unhappiness or death. She decided it's in not learning self-discipline that one turns to a life of crime or allows temptations to take over. Then one must live by always looking over the shoulder, defending oneself before the law, wondering when the next attacker will be smarter or stronger than yourself, etc.

Lisa compared it to driving within the speed limit. When exceeding the posted speed, one must always be watching to see if a patrol car is sitting hidden around the next corner. However, if one stays within the legal limit, one can concentrate on driving and not worry about speeding tickets.

Proverbs 5:22-23 says it well: "The evil deeds of a wicked man ensnare him; the cords of his sin hold him fast. He will die for lack of discipline, led astray by his own great folly." We see how David's sons, Absalom and Amnon, died because of their folly. We have only to look around us today to see the misery caused by alcohol-related car accidents, AIDS usually brought on by promiscuity or drugs, robberies, stabbings, etc., all a result of not disciplining self to stay away from the very first temptations.

Yes, Lisa realized it's love that makes a parent continue to discipline and teach a value system when sometimes it would be easier to shrug one's shoulders and look the other way.

Lisa decided to talk about discipline with Dorothy, a child psychologist who happened to be a member of her church. The conversation led to the two of them planning a Saturday morning when Dorothy would present a mini-seminar on the subject for as many parents as wished to come. In the meantime, Dorothy gave Lisa the following key points:

1. Parents, be united in purpose and philosophy.

"What do you mean by that?" Lisa asked.

"Children are masters at dividing and conquering," Dorothy explained. "They will play one parent against the other. So it's important for you and your husband to know ahead of time that you will make a habit of consulting one another; that you will settle differences of opinion out of earshot of the children."

2. Be consistent.

Lisa laughed, "You mean be consistent in our inconsistencies?"

"Yes," replied Dorothy.

3. Be firm but loving.

"What do you mean?"

"Let the child know you mean business. That 'no' means 'no,'" not 'maybe, if you beg long enough.'"

4. Understand that you will sin. Be willing to seek forgiveness from your child when that happens.

5. Set a good example. What you do often speaks more loudly than what you say.

Lisa thought a moment. "David was often a poor example to his children, wasn't he?"

Dorothy agreed. "But David was a good example in his devotion to Jehovah God. It's just that the naturally sinful self will choose to follow the path of least resistance and what appears to be 'fun.'"

6. Be sure your children get spiritual training—both at home and with the help of your church.

Lisa said, "I see many parents who send their children to Sunday school each week. You don't think that's enough?"

Dorothy shook her head. "No. Their example, first of all, is saying Sunday school is for children. "As soon as you're grown up you, too, can drink coffee and stay home on Sunday mornings." Those parents need to be participating in Sunday school with their children and then talking about the lessons at home. It reinforces what was taught that morning."

Dorothy quoted from Chuck Swindoll's book <u>The Strong Family</u>: "Effective family life does not just happen; it's the result of deliberate intention, determination, and practice." Then she added, "And a lot of sweat, tears, and prayer, too."

CHAPTER SEVENTEEN
BIBLE STUDY AND DISCUSSION

Read and discuss 2 Samuel 12 & 13. This Scripture reads like a soap opera. Why did it happen?

> ... Then Nathan said to David, "You are the man! This is what the Lord, the God of Israel, says: 'I anointed you king over Israel, and I delivered you from the hand of Saul. 8 I gave your master's house to you, and your master's wives into your arms. I gave you the house of Israel and Judah. And if all this had been too little, I would have given you even more. 9 Why did you despise the word of the Lord by doing what is evil in his eyes? You struck down Uriah with the sword of the Ammonites. 10 Now, therefore, the sword will never depart from your house, because you despised me and took the wife of Uriah the Hittite to be your own. This is what the Lord says: 'Out of your own household I am going to bring calamity upon you.'" (2 Samuel 12:7-11a)

> But when she took it to him to eat, he grabbed her and said, "Come to bed with me, my sister."
> 12 "Don't, my brother!" She said to him. "Don't force me. Such a thing should not be done in Israel." (2 Samuel 13:11-12)

CHAPTER SEVENTEEN QUESTIONS

1. List the major concepts Lisa gleaned from looking hard at David's parenting skills.

    a. _____

    b. _____

    c. _____

    d. _____

2. Do you see any evidence of favoritism as David deals with his children? How?

    _____

    _____

3. How can favoritism hurt family relationships?

    _____

    _____

    _____

4. On a scale of one to ten (one being bad and ten best), decide how you would rate David's family from dysfunctional to functional. (Read 1 Kings 2:23-25 for added information.)

    _____

5. Why did you give the numerical rating you gave to question 4 above?

6. What happens to children in dysfunctional family situations?

_____

_____

_____

The early Puritans of our country knew very well that authority, whether temporal or spiritual, begins in the home. Cotton Mather of that time said, "Well-ordered families naturally produce a good order in society." His contemporary James Fitch followed with, "Such as families are, such at last the Church and Commonwealth must be." (The Light and the Glory, by Marshall and Manuel, p. 182)

7. What specifically can you do to encourage well-ordered families in your community?

   a. Name two things within your own family unit. You may use grandchildren or nieces and nephews if you have no children directly under your roof.

      1). _____

      2). _____

b. Now name two ideas for the neighborhood which would help in creating well-ordered families. (Remember, you can't always fix everything with dollars alone.)

1) _____

2) _____

Chapter Eighteen
FAMILY OF THE COVENANT

The great stabilizer for a spiritually widowed wife is the knowledge that her husband and children are under the covenant of God. This means that God looks at your family the way he would any Christian family and gives it many blessings.

First Corinthians 7:14 says, "For the unbelieving husband has been sanctified through his wife, and the unbelieving wife has been sanctified through her believing husband. Otherwise your children would be unclean, but as it is, they are holy."

Your children are holy. This means they are set apart, special. The covenant that makes them holy was first given in Genesis 17:7: "I will establish my covenant as an everlasting covenant between me and you and your descendants after you for the generations to come, to be your God and the God of your descendants after you." (Emphasis added)

THE PROMISE OR COVENANT OF GOD

This promise or covenant flows through the Old Testament to the New. In the New Testament, the covenant is elaborated upon in Hebrews 8:10-13:

> This is the covenant I will make with the house of Israel after that time, declares the Lord. I will put my laws in their minds and write them on their hearts. I will be their God, and they will be my people. No longer will a man teach his neighbor, or a man his brother, saying, "Know the Lord,"

229

because they will know me, from the least of them to the greatest. For I will forgive their wickedness and will remember their sins no more. (emphasis added)

It is further explained in Galatians 3:14: "He redeemed us in order that the blessing given to Abraham might come to the Gentiles through Christ Jesus, so that by faith we might receive the promise of the spirit."

In Acts 2:39, Peter says you have a right to claim this promise for your family. He says, "The promise is for you and your children and for all who are far off—for all whom the Lord our God will call."

REAPING THE BENEFITS

Your husband reaps the benefit of being under the umbrella of God's covenant too. In the Old Testament, some Israelites believed and some did not as they trekked across the desert to the Promised Land. Yet all of them received manna, water, and God's blessings. So, too, your unbelieving spouse is covered in God's covenant. As long as your husband is married to you, he receives the blessings of a Christian home. He meets godly people. He has the gifts of the church bestowed upon his family and the saints pray for him. Also, you, his wife, claim the promise of the new covenant. 1 Corinthians 7:16a states, "How do you know wife, whether you will save your husband?"

When you claim the promise, God hears. As a Christian woman, you look to the Covenant Keeper and depend on Him. You submit to His will.

You trust that God will change your husbands and children's hearts and that they will know God and their Saviour, Jesus Christ.

HOW TO APPLY THE COVENANT

Now let's see how the covenant practically applies to your life.

Cheri walked to her little hideaway in the garden. She'd blown it now. When her husband encouraged her children to forget God and subtlety undermined their faith, she was devastated. No one respected her for her tirade. She was so angry and afraid. How could he do such a thing?

She sat among the azaleas and turned to the Scripture for the day. She found it in Lamentations 5:16-22. It was a description of the godly's anguish over the sins of the people.

Matthew Henry's Commentary says concerning this verse, "Nothing lies so heavily upon the spirits of good people as that which threatens the ruin of religion or weakens its interest, and it is a comfort if we can appeal to God."

Cheri thought about that. People over 2,000 years ago felt frustrated and anguished as she did. It helped to know that others felt the same way. Her precious children—she wanted them to be godly people. She didn't want their faith undermined.

Instead of panicking, Cheri needed to trust in God who reigns. "Restore us to yourself, O Lord" (Lamentations 5:21), she read. Indeed, that was her comfort. <u>Instead of looking at her husband she'd look to God and His</u> <u>covenant</u>.

You, too, can have confidence in God's covenant for your family. You already have covenant blessings. Now pray for its center—your family's salvation. Be willing to submit to His will, but center on hope.

VERSES OF HOPE

"Wives in the same way be submissive to your husband so that, if any of them do not believe the word, they may be won over without talk by the behavior of their wives, when they see the purity and reverence of your lives." (1 Peter 3:1-2)

Reason for staying: "How do you know, wife, whether you will save your husband?
(1 Corinthians 7:16a)

"They replied, 'Believe in the Lord Jesus, and you will be saved—you and your household'" (Acts 16:31)

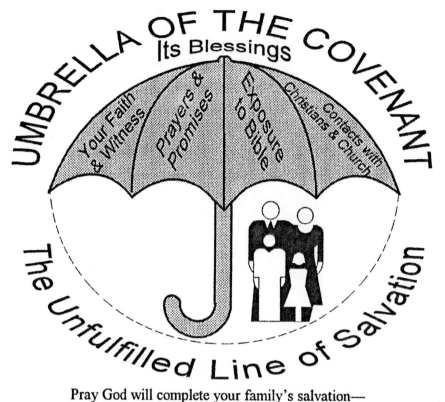

**Pray God will complete your family's salvation—
Claim the promises!**

Cheri took time to cry out to God for her family's salvation. Like the widow she came to God every day persistently asking for their salvation. She knew her great God was able to save. Obediently and humbly she asked, relying on His mercy. Then she was better able to solve problems because she trusted in God and didn't worry. She trusted that God's way was best even though she didn't understand it and concentrated on doing her part.

Rosemarie D. Malroy

BALANCE

| Confidence in God's Covenant so you are not afraid (Acts 2:39) | Willingness to cry out and beseech God to save all your family (Luke 18:1-7) |

CHAPTER EIGHTEEN
BIBLE STUDY AND DISCUSSION

Read and discuss the Scripture. How often do you think we should pray for our loved ones?

> Then Jesus told his disciples a parable to show them that they should always pray and not give up. 2 He said: "In a certain town there was a judge who neither feared God nor cared about men. 3 And there was a widow in that town who kept coming to him with the plea, 'Grant me justice against my adversary.'
>
> For some time he refused. But finally he said to himself, 'Even though I don't fear God or care about men, 5 yet because this widow keeps bothering me, I will see that she gets justice, so that she won't eventually wear me out with her coming!'"
>
> 6 And the Lord said, "Listen to what the unjust judge says. 7 And will not God bring about justice for his chosen ones, who cry out to him day and night? Will he keep putting them off? 8 I tell you, he will see that they get justice, and quickly. (Luke 18:1-8a)
>
> The promise is for you and your children and for all who are far off—for all whom the Lord our God will call. (Acts 2:39)

PROMISES I CLAIM

1. _____

_____

_____

_____

2. _____

Rosemarie D. Malroy

_____

_____

_____

3. _____

_____

_____

_____

CHAPTER EIGHTEEN QUESTIONS

1. What was the purpose of this parable of Jesus?

   _____

   _____

2. Can God use unjust men to perform justice?

   _____

3. Why did the widow come so often to the judge with her request?

   _____

   _____

4. When should you cry out to God?

   _____

5. In Acts 2:39 what is the promise? (Hebrews 8:10-13)

   _____

6. To whom is the promise given?

   _____

7. When you get discouraged with your husband and feel he will never believe, what are you to do?

   _____

   _____

8. Enumerate some of the covenant blessings your husband and children are receiving right now.

    _____

    _____

    _____

9. After you do what God asks regarding your family, why shouldn't you worry about them?

    _____

10. What part does your faith and God's sovereignty play in your ability not to worry?

    _____

    _____

Chapter Nineteen
HOPE AND HAPPINESS,
SILVER AND GOLD

A spiritually widowed wife's life may be tinged with night, but the sterling silver shines through. Your happiness is based on God. His covenant and promises uplift you, and His character gives you hope. Your sovereign God possesses all power in heaven and earth. No one defeats His counsels, overrides His purpose, or resists His will. Such a God is the one you go to each morning.

> Yours, O Lord, is the greatness and the power and the glory and the majesty and the splendor, for everything in heaven and earth is yours. Yours, O Lord, is the kingdom: you are exalted as head over all. (1 Chronicles 29:11)

THANKFULNESS LEADS TO HAPPINESS

If you sing and praise God for who He is and be thankful, happiness comes. In Psalm 77 David experiences this truth. He starts out very unhappy. He complains in verse 7, "Will the Lord reject forever?" Then he remembers God's deeds of old: "Yes, I will remember your miracles of long ago." (v. 10)

When he remembered God's good deeds, he soon sings with joy, "What god is so great as our God?" (v. 13)

Psalm 77 is a good chapter to study when you are down. You can use David's formula:

Complain to God (tell Him your troubles)

\+   Remember His past deeds (also answered prayers)

\=   Thankfulness, Joy, and Happiness

This happiness is not like the happiness from receiving a new dress. It is a happiness of the soul that makes Christians unique. It is a joy that is the best witness you can give.

CONTENTMENT MAKES FOR HAPPINESS

How can you be content when sometimes you have so many trials and tribulations? Cheri wished for more happiness and decided part of her trouble was lack of contentment. She came to the conclusion that society often feeds the fuel of our discontent. She made an interesting observation after meeting people from poorer parts of the world. She said, "The more God gives us, the less we appreciate it, and the more we concentrate on our 'unhappiness.'"

Cheri felt getting back to basics might help. She established a bottom line for necessities, so she wouldn't be so demanding. She made a list of basics. If they were met, she decided she would be content. It pleased her to fly in the face of society and choose her own contentment.

NECESSITIES

Income
Bottom Line: Enough for basic bills and needs.

Food
Bottom Line: Adequate food to keep my family and me healthy.

Clothing
Bottom Line: Enough clothing to permit us to be appropriately dressed for the occasion.

Shelter
Bottom Line: A place to shelter us from the elements keeping us comfortable and safe.

Home
Bottom Line: Having it so I can make it a happy place to be and use my talents to make it a better place.

Recreation
Bottom Line: Having some outlet to meet creative and social needs, allowing us to refresh. (Our choices: church activities, library, park service recreations, school activities, children's sports.)

Relationships
Bottom Line: A special, unique, and individual relationship with God. She found when God filled this need, all other relationships were richer. She did not demand as much of others and it freed her to enjoy them more.

Cheri found she had a great deal above "the bottom line." That helped her to be content in spite of her inclination to always want the "best." She realized the best was to be content. How do you handle contentment?

YOUR BOTTOM LINES

Income	_____
Food	_____
Clothing	_____
Shelter	_____
Home	_____
Recreation	_____
Relationships	_____

Corrie ten Boom didn't have those bottom lines. She was trying to survive in prison. She found that one of the fruits of the Spirit is joy. She depended on the Holy Spirit to fill her with love and joy despite the terrible conditions. She trusted day by day for joy in the midst of the most desperate surroundings, even when her life hung in the balance.

LAUGHTER, A GREAT ASSET

A widowed wife has much for which to be happy. God is on her side, her family is under His covenant, and she claims His promises. She appreciates God's gifts and enjoys her church, family, and friends. She loves her husband and she also has hope. So be free. Laugh. Find the funny things in life and laugh. Laugh at the ridiculous. In humor, the bittersweet usually brings forth laughter. You have a lot to laugh about.

Lisa drove home and met Todd at the door returning from his college classes. "I'll hurry and get dinner so you won't be late for your game," she said. Then she stopped. The kitchen and living room had two inches of water slushing everywhere.

"Mom, look. Can you believe this?"

"The dishwasher broke," cried Lisa. "I left it on." Lisa felt like crying. Suddenly Todd started laughing. "It's such a terrible mess. It'll take days to clean up."

Lisa looked at him standing there in the water laughing. Suddenly she started to laugh too. They both laughed until they cried. It was so terrible—so silly, but laughing felt a lot better than crying.

SARAH'S LAUGHTER

Sarah laughed too. Maybe you shouldn't laugh like she did. She laughed at God's promise. It got her in trouble. When the angels came and told her husband she'd have a son when she was in her nineties, she laughed. She had tried different tricks to see that God kept His promise. How was Abraham going to have descendants that numbered the sand of the sea when she couldn't conceive? So she tried a surrogate mother and what trouble. Now in her nineties God says she's going to have a baby. She laughed. She had given up hope that God would keep His promise. But our dear Lord, in spite of it all, kept His promise. Sarah bore Isaac, whose ancestral line produced Jesus Christ.

"And Sarah said, 'God hath made me to laugh, so that all that hear will laugh with me.'" (Genesis 21:6)

What a wonderful reason to laugh with Sarah.

GOD KEEPS HIS PROMISES

The almighty, unchangeable God of the Bible keeps His promises. And they are there in the Bible for you. As you have your quiet time with God and study His Word, you will find special promises you can claim.

Charles Spurgeon calls attention to the stability of God's promises:

> It is a cause of much weakness to many that they do not treat the promises of God as realities. If a friend makes a promise, they regard it as a substantial thing, and look for that which it secures: but the declarations of God are often viewed as so many words which mean very little.
> This is most dishonoring to the Lord, and very injurious to ourselves. Rest assured that the Lord never trifles with words. Hath he said, and will he not do it? His engagements are always kept..."

Can an instance be found in which our God has been false to His Word?

THE MYSTERY OF GOD AND HOPE

We believe God is good and has our best interest at heart. We believe God hears our cries and answers our prayers in due time in His way. However, we also must be realistic. Sin doesn't pay. Often we make our own problems. Then we can expect to receive correction from God. When we break God's commandments that He made to keep us out of trouble, we can expect to reap some trials. It is our training ground. Hope will get us through. How God will deal with us is a mystery.

"But in this case I didn't do anything wrong," Cheri said. "Why hasn't God answered my prayer?"

Perhaps Cheri had a "no" answer or a "not now" answer. Corrie ten Boom addresses that problem in her book He Sets the Captives Free. When Corrie and her sister, Betsie, were in the prison together, she prayed for her sister to get well. Betsie died.

"Why, Lord?" Corrie questioned. As she left the prison, she found that though they released her, Betsie would have remained there. Corrie thanked God that He spared Betsie that awful fate. How terrible it would have been for her to be free and her dear, dear sister suffering in prison.

God works in mysteries that we often don't understand. J. I. Packer, in his book Knowing God, says:

> For the truth is that God in His wisdom, to make and keep us humble and to teach us to walk by faith, has hidden from us almost everything that we should like to know about the providential purposes which He is working out in the churches and in our own lives. "As you do not know the path of the wind, or how the body is formed in a mother's womb, so you cannot understand the work of God, the Maker of all things." (Ecclesiastes 11:5, p. 96)

> My life is but a weaving between my God and me,
> I do not choose the colors, He worketh steadily.
> Ofttimes He weaveth sorrow and I in foolish pride,

Forgets He sees the upper, and I the underside.
(Quoted in <u>He Sets the Captives Free</u>, p. 48, by Grant Colfax Tullar)

When we deal with a sovereign God, we can trust Him for His great wisdom.

GOD ANSWERS PRAYER

Lisa sat numb from the past events. Craig had told her he felt strange. She noticed he looked rather pale—not his bouncy old self. His 55 years had never slowed him down before.

"Maybe you'd better go to the hospital," she cautiously suggested.

"Yes," he agreed. Now she marveled that he would do so. Surely the God of heaven moved him.

In the emergency room they strapped him down and tested his heart. "He's okay," the doctor told Lisa. "Probably a little heartburn. He can go home."

The doctor and nurse left the room and Craig started to get up. "Wait," he said. "I'm ... I'm fainting."

All that happened in the next few minutes blurred in Lisa's mind. The doctors prevented a major heart attack and now Craig was waiting to go to surgery. He needed a five-way bypass.

He lay there looking helpless. His eyes flickered and he reached out to her. His voice was gruff. "I've got to tell you something so you won't worry," he said. "I know you'll worry if I don't tell you and I don't make it."

He hesitated. "I trust in Jesus as my Savior ..." His voice trailed off. "I wanted you to know."

It was so simple. Lisa had waited thirty years to hear him say that. She felt no emotion. It was like a dream.

As they wheeled him off for surgery, their son Todd joined her. "All we can do is pray, Mom," he said.

The wait was long—exceedingly long. Finally a nurse came to them. "Everything is fine, Lisa. Just taking longer."

Lisa looked at the nurse. Why it was Mr. Cotter. He was a Christian, and he was assisting Craig's surgery. It was like a message from God reminding her He was in control of every detail. Imagine, in this huge city, Mr. Cotter helping Craig.

"Todd, do you remember when we had Mr. Cotter to dinner when he first came to town?"

"Yes, I remember it now. It's been a while back. Hope you gave him a good dinner," he said, chuckling.

Lisa laughed. Joy began to dance in her heart. Silver had turned to gold. The full circle completed the covenant. God answered her prayer. Joy had come in the morning.

CHAPTER NINETEEN
BIBLE STUDY AND DISCUSSION

Read Scripture and discuss.

> I cried out to God for help;
> I cried out to God to hear me.
> 2 When I was in distress, I sought the Lord;
> at night I stretched out untiring hands
> and my soul refused to be comforted.
>
> 3 I remembered you, O God, and I groaned;
> I mused, and my spirit grew faint.
> 4 You kept my eyes from closing;
> I was too troubled to speak.
> 5 I thought about the former days,
> the years of long ago;
> 6 I remembered my songs in the night.
> My heart mused and my spirit inquired:
>
> 7"Will the Lord reject us forever:
> Will he never show his favor again?
> 8 Has his unfailing love vanished forever?
> Has his promise failed for all time?
> 9 Has God forgotten to be merciful?
> Has he in anger withheld his compassion?"
>
> 10 Then I thought, "To this I will appeal:
> the years of the right hand of the Most High."
> 11 I will remember the deeds of the Lord:
> yes,I will remember your miracles of
> long ago.
> 12 I will meditate on all your works
> and consider all your mighty deeds.
>
> 13 Your ways, O God, are holy.
> What god is so great as our God?
> 14 You are the God who performs miracles;
> you display your power among the peoples.
> 15 With your mighty arm you redeemed

your people,
the descendants of Jacob and Joseph. (Psalm 77:1-15a)

CHAPTER NINETEEN QUESTIONS

1. What was the first thing David did in Psalm 77?

    _____

2. How did he feel?

    _____

3. What questions did he ask?

    _____

    _____

    _____

4. What did he remember?

    _____

    _____

5. As soon as he started meditating on God's deeds, what happened? Did his faith increase?

    _____

6. David started out depressed in this Psalm. How did he end?

    _____

7. How did he express God's sovereignty and greatness?

Rosemarie D. Malroy

8. Tell of one incident when God answered your prayer in a special way.

_____

_____

_____

9. Does remembering answered prayer encourage you and give you hope?

_____

How does it help you to praise Him?

_____

10. Memorize your favorite verse with a promise. Depend on God to answer it. Trust in God to keep His covenant with you. Then enjoy life and praise Him for all good things. May God bless you and grant you the desires of your heart. May your desires be His.

MY FAVORITE PROMISES

ON WHICH I CENTER MY LIFE

_____

_____

250

Rosemarie D. Malroy

WORKS CITED

Chapter 2   From Forgiven to Forgiving
                 Jay Adams
                 Calvary Press, Box 805 Amityville, NY11701 1994

Chapter 3   Seven Minutes With God
                 Robert D. Foster
                 Navpress, P.O. Box 20, Colorado Springs, CO 80901

Chapter 9   George MacDonald, 365 Readings, Troubled Soul, p. 18
                 Edited by C. S. Lewis, MacMillan, 1947

Chapter 10   Tabletalk, Ligonier Ministries,
                 Hard Cases, Terry Johnson, August 1994

                 Fundamentalist Journal
                 The Unheard Screams of Private Violence
                 Lois Hoadley Dick, October 1989

                 Fundamentalist Journal
                 Leading Victims to Victory
                 Ronald E. Hawkins, October 1989

                 Parade Magazine
                 Arrest the Wife Beaters, October 1983

                 Focus on the Family
                 Living with a Controller
                 Tim Kimmel, June 1993, p. 6

                 The Presbyterian Journal
                 Christ and Battered Wives
                 Maxinne V. Hoffman, April 1983

                 Rain, by Shirley S. Miller

                 George MacDonald, 365 Readings [61] Knowledge, p. 28
                 Collected by C. S. Lewis, MacMillan, 1947

Chapter 11   The Hidden Treasure in Suffering, p. 96
              Basilea Schlink, Evangelical Sisterhood of Mary
              P.O.B. 13 01 29, D 6100 Darmstadt 13, West Germany

              The Four Loves, p. 177
              C. S. Lewis

Chapter 13   The Biblical View of Self-Esteem, Self-Love, Self-Image
              Jay E. Adams
              Harvest House Publishers, 1986

              The Great Divorce, p. 6
              C. S. Lewis

              Putting Humpty Dumpty Together Again
              Sylvia D. Burke
              1st Books Library www.1stbooks.com

Chapter 15   The Christian Family
              Larry Christenson
              Bethany Fellowship, 1970

              It's My Turn
              Ruth Bell Graham
              Fleming H. Revell Company, 1982

Chapter 17   The Parenting Bible
              Zondervan Publishing, 1994

              The Strong Family
              Chuck Swindoll
              Zondervan Publishing, 1994

Chapter 19   A Harvest
              HBJ Book, 1960
              Harcourt Brace Jovanovich Publishers

              He Sets the Captives Free
              Corrie ten Boom
              Fleming H. Revell Company, 1977

              Knowing God

J. I. Packer
InterVarsity Press, 1973

Morning and Evening
Charles Haddon Spurgeon

Rosemarie D. Malroy

ABOUT THE AUTHOR

Rosemarie Malroy's life experiences give her an unusual sensitivity for spiritually widowed wives. Mother of three children, she has lived in Washington, Montana, Virginia and Arizona—wherever her husband's professional forestry job led them. Living in remote areas of an Indian reservation to a Washington D.C. suburb, she met Christian women, like herself, married to unbelieving men or those unwilling to take any Christian leadership. She found, whatever their circumstances, these women all had the same basic problems. Rosemarie started Bible studies and together the women provided spiritual support for each other. Their lives are shared in her book. Some of the husbands are now Christians.

Over the years, the author kept notes from her personal Bible study. These notes are the basis for *Spiritually Widowed Wives*. She is convinced when a woman comes to God and listens to His Word, God will be her spiritual husband who leads and balances her life.

She can be reached by e-mail: rosemalroy@cox.net

Printed in the United States
837600002B

9 781403 322326